Best Wishes

Geoff

The **Performance** CONNECTION

A powerful new system for aligning
purpose, identity and performance
in the workplace

DENNIS DEWILDE
& Geoff Anderson

1ˢᵗ edition, 2006

 WalkervillePublishing

Published by
Walkerville Publishing Inc.

First Printing: September, 2006
Printed in China by Everbest Printing Co., Ltd.

International Standard Book Number: 0-9731834-7-0

Catalogue In Publication Data

DeWilde, Dennis, 1950-
          The performance connection / Dennis DeWilde, Geoff Anderson.

ISBN 0-9731834-7-0

          1. Management. I. Anderson, Geoff, 1955- II. Title.

HD31.D497 2006   658.4   C2006-902768-4

Printed in China
Walkerville Publishing Inc.
Suite 201-420 Devonshire Road
Windsor ON N8Y 4T6
www.walkerville.com

Preface

Why do some employees nearly always do the right thing at the right time? How do they consistently create individual solutions that fit so well into the "big picture"? Why do they act while others await direction! What makes these employees so accountable and responsible? Such employees make our jobs so easy that we wish everyone would work like them.

Have you ever had a boss who made you feel like you could handle any situation? You go into their office with a problem and emerge with your solution! Beaming about your problem-solving ability, you rush excitedly to put "your" solution into action. You feel so special that you just know you can handle even the most difficult of problems!

I've had both this kind of employees and this kind of boss – even been both – and have spent more than 25 years coaching people on how to create these situations to improve performance. During this time, I have witnessed organizations try just about every process improvement and empowerment technique imaginable, which all looked so promising at the start and made so little difference in the end. Over time, it became obvious that something significant was being missed. Either it was all about the people or it was all about the business, and the two were often not compatible. When I began working on organizational design, it quickly became evident that my approach to organizational process and leadership is based upon a unique philosophy that allows both individual needs and business performance demands to not only co-exist but to support one another. In listening to and applying this approach, most leaders found it insightful albeit unorthodox wisdom, causing regular questions about the underlying framework. Having written several short papers describing pieces of the process, it seemed time to describe the whole concept in readable and readily applicable terms.

For assistance in putting this organizational process into book form, I turned to Geoff Anderson, a colleague who has worked with me in developing and implementing this concept internationally. His perception and ability to clarify thoughts had previously helped me shape the concept and to turn theory into reality and then into results. He was for me the obvious co-author.

We wrote this book to help leaders discover tools to address the fundamental problems inherent in traditional management processes where the needs of leaders and workers are subordinated to corporate performance demands. *The Performance Connection* is a *how-to* book for developing a high-performing organization by integrating our human relational needs for **purpose**, **identity**, and **accountability** into the organizational and leadership processes. For all those leaders out there who are frustrated by lack of employee engagement and commitment, the Relational Management Model introduced in this book supplies the missing piece of the puzzle to release the promise of all those leadership techniques and employee training programs that you have tried and that have thus far failed to deliver the miracle of human creativity.

The Performance Connection is a book for leaders who want both performance *and* people to grow in our world of rapid change and constant performance challenges.

Dennis DeWilde

How This Book is Structured

An overview of the Relational Management Model, using purpose, identity, and accountability to connect Me Inc. and Business Inc. thru acknowledgement of the three relational laws of life:
> *Possibilities Align Actions,*
> *Contribution Defines Relationships, and*
> *Competition Sets the Standards.*

A guide for using the talents and skills of a leader to bring responsibility into the workplace by using the four Relational Leadership Practices:
> *From End to Start,*
> *Enable Responsibility,*
> *Be in Learning, and*
> *Involve Others in the Conversation.*

How Vision and Strategic Intent are integrated into the Relational Management Model to create a Living Performance Vision as the guide for decision making and action within the organization.

How to build a business-purpose team organizational structure that connects Strategic Intent and Me Inc. to develop internal enterprises and introduce free-market concepts into organizations.

How accountability principles are used for cascading Strategic Intent and linking the organization to its performance goals and to each other.

The business processes for integrating strategy, planning, accountability, and compensation in the normal course of business management.

The implementation steps for transitioning the Relational Management Model into an organization.

Table of Contents

Introduction

It's Personal
and It's Business

The Need to Connect ...

Every business or enterprise, including a growing number of not-for-profit organizations struggling to exist in today's challenging environment, must succeed at one common, overarching issue: *The need to create a connection between employees and the performance demands of their business.*

When creating this connection between people and organizational performance, every enterprise must deal with the *change factor*. The change factor is code for natural evolution, which is increasingly accelerated by a digital catalyst. This digital catalyst allows codification of knowledge and facilitates nearly instantaneous communication. Such rapid information transfer and assimilation intensifies competitive pressures and creates constantly changing performance demands. In other words, the needs of the business are increasingly dynamic.

What is also not news to anyone in a management position is that the needs of the individual, which are also dynamic, have changed dramatically – or perhaps we should say progressed – since the industrialization of society. The needs of the individual have progressed beyond *basic[1]* needs for food, shelter, and survival because society largely guarantees these needs. Instead, the needs of individuals today are largely *relational* – social factors, recognition, and creative expression.

How have we, under industrial society's organizational-man model, responded to these changing needs – both the changing needs of the company and the individual? In true business-school fashion, we introduced a buzzword – value-creation – as the driver for altering the business models required for success.

On the company side, the pre-1990s employment model – direct hire, annual raises, retirement guarantees, generous benefits, security and etc., all in exchange for commitment – became obsolete as global competition (whether from the products themselves or global ideas transferred into local competition) entered the picture. Flying a banner saying "Value creation resides in human nature," companies incentivized and empowered, outsourced and downsized. "It's not personal, it's business!" has become a common refrain.

For the individual, the concept variously labeled Brand You,[2] Individual Inc., or Me Inc. stressed that the era of depending on the corporation for career development is a thing of the past. The concept in a nutshell is that the individual is tantamount to a business and must think and operate like a business – complete with his or her own value-creation strategy, business model, product identification, and etc.

The inevitable outcome of these diverging responses has been an increase in the tension between business needs and employee needs. As each party moved to a more independent state of being, the connections between people and the performance demands of the business have become more, not less, difficult to manage – and the ever-increasing demands of the marketplace relative to the needs of the individual make it increasingly difficult for managers to bridge this ever-widening gap. Business schools and consultants advise organizations on various techniques to span this chasm, but what has not been offered is a fundamental change in the organizational model, or contextual paradigm, that underpins business management.

We still operate under the same motivational model that was used before this rapid shift in the marketplace and in employee needs. If you don't believe us, simply answer the following questions: Do you have, or wish you had, some form of incentive compensation or pay-for-performance

*Hey! Could **WE** care about Business Inc. too?*

scheme? Have you ever promised someone who works for you a raise, bonus, promotion, or any other carrot, in exchange for meeting a goal? Have you ever threatened (actually or implied) someone who works for you with dismissal or demotion if they failed to perform? Do you view the finance department as a control body?

Whether we like to admit it or not, we still largely rely on the "carrot-and-stick" model and its implementation tool – "command-and-control" management. This in spite of the fact that it has been politically incorrect to be seen as a command-and-control type of leader for some 25 years. When you visualize this carrot-and-stick philosophy, what is usually depicted as being between the carrot-and-stick? Maybe the image this model uses as a metaphor should indicate that this is not the best methodology for addressing human relational needs in the 21st century.

We are not saying that the carrot-and-stick is utterly wrong, however. Human needs are hierarchical and move up and down a needs pyramid depending on the individual's perception of each particular situation. As noted above, the social structure largely provides for the fulfillment of an individual's basic needs, but those needs remain in play in many circumstances, making the old paradigm moderately functional. However, merely addressing the basic needs of employees is a necessary but not sufficient condition for success. In short, the carrot-and-stick/command-and-control model is incomplete.

Today, organizations require a more dynamic model – one that meets the **needs of Business Inc., the organization**, *and* the **needs of Me Inc., the** *individual.* In other words, a model that responds to the changes in both aspects of the modern organization. However, organizations still require a model that will allow for command-and-control when the situation demands that type of response even as the model evolves beyond command-and-control's constraints to engage the individual in a relationship with the performance vision of the organization. What we are suggesting is a model that addresses human relational *and* business performance needs simultaneously, so that both will thrive in today's dynamic world.

We developed *The Performance Connection* to address this issue, and within these pages you will find a new approach to organizational management using a relational needs framework

... in a Relational Way.

The starting premise for this book was an obvious correlation: A relational world requires a relational model for organizational management. This new model starts with an understanding, and alignment, of relational elements for organizations and for people: *Purpose, Identity,* and *Accountability.*[3]

Purpose, for individuals, is our reason for existing. It is what drives us, why we are here, and what we strive to achieve. It is the source of our passions and commitments. Purpose engages the *heart*[4] for the energy to apply our uniqueness to creative ends. In a spiritual sense, purpose is our relationship with the higher "Being," God, Yahweh, Allah, the Force, however you care to state it.

For an organization, purpose is its mission and the value it provides to society. Purpose is the foundation of the organization's *Vision*.

- *Identity, for individuals,* is our uniqueness. In its fullest and perhaps most confusing sense, our identity consists of our individual, distinguishing characteristics within our societal group. It is our individual view of the world, and reciprocally, our interpretation of ourselves in that world as both are shaped by our cultural, community, and family history and our distinct talents. Identity is about our relationship with our self – it is who we think we are. For individuals, identity gives the *head* a clear understanding of self-worth and provides the strength to persevere.

For an organization, identity is what that enterprise does exceptionally well. Identity is how the organization defines itself, and it is the foundation for the organization's **Strategy**.

- **Accountability,** *for individuals,* is our mark in the sands of time. It is our level of responsibility for the impact, or results, within a relationship. Accountability is ownership of our actions and decisions. It allows the adult in us to embrace the responsibilities that come with choice. For individuals, accountability sets the *hands* in motion toward our purposeful ends.

   For an organization, accountability is measured through the results achieved relative to the organization's **Performance Goals.**

For the individual, the three relational elements *(**Purpose, Identity,** and **Accountability**)* are what we offer to the world.

For an organization, these three relational elements *(**Vision, Strategy,** and **Performance Goals**)* are expressed as the **Performance Vision** of the enterprise – the organization's statement of its relational desires with all stakeholders.

For the organization *and* the individual, it is the balance of all three elements that allows for success. Too much focus on **Purpose** or **Vision**, and we lack traction to move forward – life is a dream with no connection to reality. Too little of these and life lacks meaning or direction.

Too much focus on **Identity** or **Strategy**, and we live within ourselves: paralysis by analysis for the business; and me, me, me for the individual. Too little of these and we have no foundation upon which to stand let alone to build.

Too much focus on **Accountability** or **Performance Goals,** and we lose sight of the big picture – resulting in individual burnout and an anything-goes-as-long-as-we-meet-the-target mentality. Too little accountability places us in a victim's world of dependency: "they" are responsible for everything – someone else is always to blame.

A basic relational law of life governs each of these three needs. Each law controls its relational element, determining the strength and balance of this three-dimensional connection.

The three relational laws of life are:

- **Possibilities Align Actions** – bringing *Purpose* and reality together.

- **Contribution Defines Relationships** – valuing *Identity*.

- **Competition Sets the Standards** – determining the level of *Accountability*.

Working simultaneously at both the individual and organizational level, each law reinforces the others, and together they connect the whole person (head, heart, and hands) to the work required.

- For the *individual*, the relational laws establish an association with the organization's performance vision by answering adequately and thereby reinforcing the validity of the following question: "What's in it for me?"

- For the *organization*, the relational laws indicate where the enterprise is going and what is needed to get there.

Adherence to these three relational laws constructs a spiral for development and growth:

- *Possibilities* pull the individual and the organization toward their purpose, providing bearings for the *how* and *why* questions the individual feels need answered.

- *Contribution* clarity lets individuals know what they bring to the relationship, providing focus, confidence, and energy for the work.

- *Competition*, as the measurement source, allows individuals to answer the question "Is it enough?" by placing accountability within his or her hands and removing the inner child's need for approval at every turn.

Let's take a look at how these laws work to reinforce one another and to support relational connectivity.

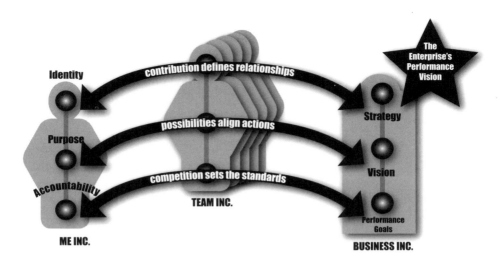

Using Possibilities to Align Actions ...

Actions follow thoughts. People's actions are consistent with their in-the-moment perception of what is possible, and they want to do the right thing. Shaped by the truths in their *hearts*, people define possibilities in every situation they encounter. Then they act to realize these perceived possibilities. This intuition is merely the subconscious recognition of possibilities in a situation as they are translated into behavior. For example, if we perceive that another person is an expert, they become the embodiment of the possibility for us to learn, and our interactions with them take on the characteristics of a teacher-student relationship. In conversation, because we are tuned into the possibilities within the situation before us, we listen to learn from experts, to collaborate with colleagues, or to level the playing field with those individuals we view as competitors. As leaders, we define people as possibilities for success or failure, and we relate to them accordingly. In short, the possibilities as we perceive them align our actions and define our relationships both in positive and in limiting ways.

The enterprise's *vision* is a statement of the business as a future possibility, or what it aspires to be. The vision is this intuition made conscious. Properly constructed and cascaded throughout the organization, the vision also serves as a guiding light to pull the organization forward. By answering an overarching question – "How does this contribute to the vision?" – the vision controls the selection and prioritization of options by business units, teams, or work groups.

The vision is also the source of possibilities for the individual employee. It is the source of the answer to the question "What's in it for me?" If the employee's only answer is money, the connection addresses only basic needs – and the employee's actions will only be about money. However, if the answer addresses their **Purpose** in life, the connection is relational – and their actions will be from the *heart*. Their actions will align with the possibilities they see in the situation.

What does this discussion of how possibilities align actions tell us about the role of leadership under this relational model? For one thing, if you tell an employee that a given task is about the money, then it will be about the money. This may be motivation enough in some cases, but there are limits to an organization's success if this is all that is at stake for the individual. However, if a manager provides vision and creates an environment wherein employees can find expression for even a small part of their passions, they will bring their *hearts* to work. Then, not only do the chances for success go up demonstrably, but the level of success that can be achieved is extended dramatically.

... while Contribution Defines Relationships

How does your business relate to its customers – price, service, value? What primary attributes do you bring to your employer – practical experience, marketing connections, innovative ideas? How does your answer shape your relationship with the organization?

Contribution is part of a corporation's or an individual's unique **Identity**. For corporations, this identity is critical to their strategy. For individuals, understanding identity strengthens relational connections.

Nike, Coke, and Ralph Lauren spend millions shaping a corporate identity, or image, in their relationship with consumers. Their identity as winners, as attractive and cool, or as the definition of style distinguishes them and their products' place in their customer's value chain. A major aspect of their contribution to their clientele, in their relationship with consumers, is precisely image, and these corporations work hard to maintain it. Yet, these firms may have an entirely different identity in their relationship with their suppliers or even their shareholders. Identity in a relationship is about what you bring to the other party.

Similarly, an individual's "Me Inc." business has a strategy that defines his or her relationship with the enterprise(s) with/for whom they work. Each individual's contribution is a consequence of their talent, knowledge, and view of life – factors that make us unique and identify us as individuals. Understanding this identity is foundational for a "Me Inc." Your Me Inc. cannot be more that who you are, but it should not be less either.

Relational leaders manage their organizations by interacting with staff, not based upon their position or job description, but based upon the contribution of each person's Me Inc. to the organization's strategy. This contribution-driven interaction softens the hard lines of organizational structure. This law makes *Business Identity Formation* the key to designing and managing organizational structure. When an organizational structure is designed to require individual teams to identify the various components of their business (products, services, and customers), the structure accepts relationships based upon contribution and drives free-market discipline and responsibility into the organization.

When employee contribution is used for organizational management, individuals gain clarity regarding what it is they deliver to the business, and thus, regarding their *identity*, their underlying talents and gifts. As *identity* becomes clear to the *head*, Me Inc. is strengthened, confidence increases, and an upward spiral of performance growth is realized.

... and Competition Sets the Standards.

In a free-market society, just as is true in the biological world, competition is an evolutionary factor – and employer and employee performance standards are a consequence. The ***Performance Goals*** for a business are a statement of what is necessary for it to succeed in this free-market environment, and it should be noted that these goals are relative benchmarks and not absolute standards. Many organizations spend their (often short) lives seemingly in ignorance of this basic law of nature. They set targets based upon improvement from past performance only to find that their competitors have left them in the dust. Based upon our positioning in the food-chain of life, standards of performance, whether professional or personal, are established by competitive forces, and our relationship to these standards is a measure of ***Accountability***.

Accountability for individuals is *not* set by managers, shareholders, or other stakeholders – although any of these may be responsible for sifting through the data and clarifying the specifics. Accountability is actually established by the forces of competition. This law throws off the shackles of the parent-child metaphor, which often dominates the management process.

It calls the adult in us to be *accountable* for the choices we make toward meeting the standards demanded by competitive forces. Understanding this dynamic reinforces individual responsibility relative to performance delivery and sets the *hands* in motion.

Organizational systems can reinforce this law. For example, a strategy-driven accountability system that uses cascaded and linked performance measures based upon the standards of competition will reinforce this law and can serve to connect accountability and identity. Labor markets ultimately must adjust to the demands of competitive pressure, and compensation practices should support the focus on competition. When thought of as inflation adjustments, annual raises do not help make this point. All business policies can either reinforce individual accountability or present themselves as legal code, resulting not in performance but an excuse for failure: "Don't blame me. I followed the policy!"

Using A Perform and Learn Culture ...

These three basic relational laws govern the Relational Management Model. They provide a new context for conventional wisdom about designing and leading organizations. These laws expand motivation beyond the carrot-and-stick, moving the enterprise beyond command-and-control and into a *Perform and Learn* culture as shown on page 27.

However, cultural transformation is more than listing changes and distinctions. Cultural transformation results from leadership practices that make a difference – simple, intuitive, common sense practices that transform these relational laws into action. *The Performance Connection* offers four categorical practices in this regard:

1. **From End to Start** – a practice of clarifying purpose as a guide for present actions. This practice puts the Possibilities Align Actions law to work, clarifying purpose and outcomes when moving into action. You can apply this practice to everything from daily organizational tasks and meeting agenda design to the formation of a new business.

2. **Enable Responsibility** – a practice for ensuring individual and collective responsibility by providing Space for others to make choices. This practice allows you to provide *Direction* – like objectives and goals – not *directives*. This practice calls for setting governance boundaries that include both "must

Area of definition	Command & Control	Perform & Learn
Leadership commitment...	Knowing what is best	Learning from everyone
Performance goals..........	Predictable increments	Stretched possibilities
Relationships.................	Hierarchical	Contribution-based
Performance standards....	Management defined	Competitively defined
Supervisory role............	Directive and judging	Direction and support
Organizational interactions	Territorial	Collaborative
Motivation	Obedience	Commitment
Individual's responsibility.	Compliance	Performance
Basis of decision making	Past Experience	Future vision
Control practices...........	Delegate & authorize	Values and performance
Conversation interactions	Opinions are truth	Opinions are views
Teaching approach.........	Expert instructions	Asking and inquiring
Cultural norm..............	Being in agreement	Authentic speaking
Scientific metaphor.........	Newtonian mechanics	Einsteinian relativity
Hierarchy of needs.........	Survival-based	Relations included
Psychological metaphor	Parent / Child	Adult to Adult

do this" and "cannot do that" categories, and then facilitates engagement, allowing you to help people understand their contribution and purpose in relation to the goals.

3. **Be in Learning** – a practice of using inquiry to expose the assumptions that define our reality. Past experience is a double-edged sword – it teaches us and it limits us. If all your today-actions are conditioned by your yesterday-experiences, your future has already occurred. To *Be in Learning* means to be open to understanding which experience-based truths lead you to false conclusions about today and the future.

4. **Involve Others in the Conversation** – a practice of appreciating the contribution of others by using questions to listen, learn, and teach. This practice is the art of using questions in communications with others, the answers to which are the thoughts you wish to convey. Communicating is about what is heard, not what is said. Listening gives you clues as to how others might hear what you have to say. If you commit to listening before you speak, others are better able to hear you.

... in an Integrated System

This Relational Management Model is not a one-dimensional solution. It takes an integrated system to build a successful organization, including industry-specific understandings to drive a strategy that focuses products and services toward specific customers. No process for creating an individual's relationship with performance (for that is what organizations must do) can be simplified down to a clear-cut recipe, as each element of organizational process – staff, style, structure, and systems – must be wrapped within strategy and integrated with the performance vision. In short, *The Performance Connection* does not contain a one-size-fits-all prescription for the relational model, but rather, strategies to implement the integrated performance connection into your enterprise.

There are four parts to this integrated performance connection concept:

- **Relational Leadership,** which acknowledges individual uniqueness, addresses relational needs, and ensures individual responsibility for maintaining a connection with the enterprise's performance vision even as competitive forces change the goals.

- **A Living Vision and Strategy,** which provides the performance vision and identifies Strategic Intent for organizational focus. These are the organization's *purpose* and *identity* statements, which together constitute the foundation upon which organizational performance is built, but these are also the foundation upon which the individual stands as a part of the organization.

- **A Business-Purpose Defined Team Structure,** which establishes an entrepreneurial, market-driven internal environment for the enterprise. Me Inc. is a free-market paradigm that is usually forced to fit into an authoritarian concept. Business-purpose designed team structures help return free-market concepts to the organization and thus enable an alignment with the Me Inc. paradigm.

- **A Strategy-Linked and Cascaded Accountability System,** which supplies tangible goals and creates the assurance framework to allow for the elimination of command-and-control style procedures. The market-driven internal environment created by the business-purpose team structure allows for meaningful *accountability* measurement (instead of authoritarian judgments) as the basis for control. Linked and cascaded measures keep the organization connected to its strategic foundation.

This Relational Management Model is based upon some "truths" that the authors feel must be listed at this point:

- The basic emotions, such as love or fear, set the context for our human interactions. For example, acting out of fear will create a fear-based response, and acting out of love will create a love-based response. Importantly for our discussion here, the emotion from which we act is a choice.

- Organizations are a collection of people and thus share the same basic traits that apply to individual humans. Relational laws that work for individuals also work for organizations.

- People want to do well – they do not want to fail – and their actions are consistent with their understanding of the possibilities presented to them. Management can better change their employees' actions by changing their possibilities rather than by trying to control or prevent the actions.

- An individual's world is shaped by his or her view of themselves as a possibility. This shows up as part of their basic talents and is complimented by, but not due to, learned skills or knowledge.

- Development of individuals is most effectively done by leveraging strengths (identity traits) rather than training to fix identified weaknesses. The better we understand our identity, the faster we are capable of growth. Fixing others is a job for psychologists, not leaders or managers.

- The laws of nature are also relationships that apply to free-markets, and in the long run, they apply to individuals and enterprises with equal force. Interdependency and competition are not mutually exclusive – both are required to survive. The more attuned organizations are to these natural free-market forces, the more efficient those organizations will be.

- The past has a strong grip on humans, both teaching us and shaping our future. We carry lessons learned from our childhood training into adult relationships – including the parenting model of leadership. As a result, we work very hard to make decisions we made yesterday look like the correct ones, even at the expense of our future goals. Our lives are greatly improved if our judgments are informed by the past but not tied to it. We have the opportunity to start each day anew, facing our future and not looking backward at our past.

- Our uniqueness is a terrible thing to waste. It is not a rule that we must lose individual identity in order to be a team player. Leaders are people too. They are unique and special – not some amalgamation of the "30 most favorable management attributes" or any other recipe for their behavior. Authenticity is far more valuable in business than game-playing. People know *where-we-are-coming-from* anyway – we cannot fake who we really are.

- There are many truths that remain unidentified and undiscovered in each of us. In fact, all truths are only a resting point on a learning curve. They are more useful as stepping-off points than as foundations.

If you believe that people need to be constantly threatened and controlled to keep them from making the wrong choices, close this book and best of luck with the success of your enterprise. If you firmly believe that information is power and must not be shared with team members, or if you do not trust anybody but yourself and believe that the carrot-and-stick model is the only true way to manage – that anything else is being soft – that is your prerogative.

Please note, however, if you continue making decisions as you have done in the past, you will keep getting the same outcomes in the future. That is why history repeats itself. If your current actions are determined entirely by your past experiences, the future has already occurred – it is the past merely masquerading under a new name called "future."

If you are still reading, you have at least a passing recognition of the innate qualities of people and a desire to increase your enterprise's performance capacity to accommodate the changing demands of the future. As you proceed, some words of warning are in order, however. Focusing on *Purpose, Identity,* and *Accountability* as the basis of healthy relationships might transform more than your business-related relationships. As you follow this relational-needs thought process, you will develop a better understanding of your own identity. It is an underlying assumption of *The Performance Connection* that this will be a good thing for both you and your enterprise, but it can be disconcerting at first. Leadership from a relational perspective requires that the "authentic you" become more available. So, if revealing the real you makes you uncomfortable, continue reading with caution.

...to Transition into the Performance Connection.

The Performance Connection is not a cookbook-type manual for performance improvement. In order to make the connection, leaders and employees must transition from the traditional method of control to a relational approach that brings the individual into a position of responsibility for his or her success within the success of the specific enterprise. This transition is not something theoretical that you apply or with which you overlay your enterprise, but rather, this transition takes place as part of our everyday lives as we go about doing the business of the organization. This is a transition in real time and involves real people. *The Performance Connection* respects the fact that organizations, like people, are works-in-progress at all times. Even if the external environmental conditions were to stand still for as long as a year, some of the people within the organization or several of its stakeholders will change during that time. Thus the framework of this book is premised upon the fact that a leader cannot stop-the-wheels that run the shop in order to reshape an organization, but rather, that transition is precisely that, an ongoing process.

The actual journey of this transition begins when leadership decides to work within a ***Perform and Learn*** cultural context. This first step may be as easy as moving from an attitude of *knowing* to an attitude of *learning*, which sometimes requires altering our past responses. We must move from "We tried that already!" to "We thought we had tried that concept, but perhaps we can learn from a different contextual approach."

This change of leadership emphasis is essential to making a performance connection, but please note: organizations cannot move directly into a perform-and-learn cultural paradigm. A command-and-control environment creates a feeling of dependency in employees, and the transition from dependency, through the independency stage, and into interdependency is an organizational maturation[5] process.

This transition to organizational maturity is the ongoing development of a collective culture wherein staff learns to take responsibility for the

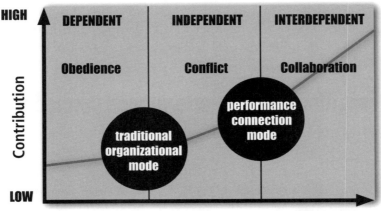

Organizational Maturity

HIGH

| DEPENDENT | INDEPENDENT | INTERDEPENDENT |

Obedience | Conflict | Collaboration

performance connection mode

traditional organizational mode

Contribution

LOW

Stages of Organizational/ Personal Maturity

"They" Stage
People place their needs at risk to others and are disappointed if their needs are not met

"I" Stage
People satisfy their own needs at the expense of others

"We" Stage
People satisfy their own needs whilst also satisfying the needs of others

impact of their actions on others – in other words learning to live collaboratively. This organizational progression requires leadership to employ transitional strategies.

The transitional success path for making a performance connection will require:

1. Clarity as regards goals that are both tangible and visionary, that answer the question "Who do we need to be?" and provide a clear statement of your Living Vision and Strategic Intent.

2. Committed leaders who understand and live relational leadership and who are energized by their Living Vision for the organization.

3. An understanding of today's realities in terms of strategic position, organizational capacity, and financial strength.

4. A process by which business teams will build commitment to the Living Vision for the enterprise.

5. An integrated accountability system that links strategy and measures processes, performance, and progress.

None of these five requirements is an independent event. They must be integrated and must progress together – this strategy must move forward on all fronts. This paradigm shift is a transition requiring new learning and understanding on the part of everyone, but especially on the part of leaders, who are required to show the way rather than to simply anoint the troops and stand aside. New tools of the trade are needed. *The Performance Connection* will provide these new tools and show you how to integrate the elements of this relational organizational management model in order to transition to a perform-and-learn culture within the enterprise.

Obviously, in order to show the way, it is useful to understand that way. The next section of this book is the leadership element of the model.

Notes

1. *Abraham H. Maslow developed the Hierarchy of Needs theory over 50 years ago. Needs progress from basic physiological and safety needs through social requirements, esteem, and actualization. It can be argued that the behavior of an individual is determined by the highest need at the moment, but that preceding needs must be somewhat satisfied before the next progressive need begins to dominate.*

2. *We are familiar with "Brand You" from the Tom Peters Company use of the term. We do not recall where we first heard the terms "Individual Inc." and "Me Inc.", although we believe they have been around for some time.*

3. *Tony Dibiasio first introduced Dennis to these three relational requirements after Dennis told him that he was struggling to find a way of expressing how the laws for organizational management helped individuals relate to the vision of the enterprise. Tony simply said: "You know, in Naomi Rosenblatt's book, **Wrestling with Angels,** she says that people need three things to be in a relationship: purpose, identity, and accountability." It hit Dennis like a rock! These were the very things he had been feeling when developing these laws. Now he had the necessary words!*

4. *James R. Ewing of Executive Arts introduced us to the term "Head, Heart, & Hands" in 1991, when he worked as an executive coach during the transformation of BP's North Sea Oil & Gas operations. Jim works to obtain alignment of these three elements through commitment of the individual to performance goals.*

5. *Author Stephen R. Covey in his best selling book, **The 7 Habits of Highly Effective People,** Simon & Schuster Inc., speaks of the Maturity Continuum as part of the natural laws of growth for individuals from infancy to adulthood. We believe that organizations can move through these same developmental stages if managed using the relational leadership model.*

It takes ME and THEE to create WE

An enterprise may begin as an idea or concept, but its ability to profit from that concept rises or falls according to the quality of its leadership. For any enterprise larger than a single-person firm, the quality of leadership can be measured by management's ability *to create a connection between their people and the performance demands of their business.* In other words, their ability to bridge the ever-growing gap between Me Inc. and Business Inc. to create We Inc., linking the performance vision of the enterprise and the individual.

Although our definition of leadership includes the art of mobilizing others into action, relational leadership does *not* start with others. Relational leadership starts with you. Relational leadership is built on a foundation of the leader as an individual, and the leader's connection with the enterprise's vision and its stakeholders. In this opening section, we will show you how relational leaders go about making these connections work.

Relational leadership allows for a leader's transformation from parent, or hero, to leader-as-adult within an organization of other adults. *The Performance Connection* presents a picture of a leader as an adult with specific responsibility for organizational direction, boundary determination, and support – never as a parent for the organization. This means that we must challenge much of the historical training about how to be a leader. At each step along the way, we must keep asking one critical question: "How do we help others be responsible?"

The piecemeal use of techniques and mini-processes that are based on concepts of individual responsibility are a start, but these efforts often get smothered within cultures that reward position power, encourage compliant behavior at the expense of performance, discourage individuality, and promote looking good rather than allowing authenticity and creativity to emerge. A more complete solution is to build a relational context by focusing on the three relational elements – *purpose, identity,* and *accountability* – using the three basic laws of relational connectivity:

- **Possibilities Align Actions** – bringing **Purpose** and reality together.

- **Contribution Defines Relationships** – valuing **Identity**.

- **Competition Sets the Standards** – determining the level of **Accountability**.

This solution also includes taking responsibility for yourself and those around you in a *perform-and-learn* culture through the application of the four leadership practices:

- **From End to Start**

- **Enable Responsibility**

- **Be in Learning**

- **Involve Others in the Conversation**

This section of the book begins with the leader's perspective – how a leader uses his or her education, background, experience, creativity, and intuition when engaging the organization. This perspective requires an understanding of oneself as a unique being, knowing how you connect to your organization's vision, and being clear about the definitions of others you hold. We then devote a chapter each to the four leadership practices.

Chapter 1

"There's only one corner of the universe you can be certain of improving, and that's your own self."
Aldous Huxley

First It's All About ME Inc.

Your best people come to you for advice, respect your input, and leave you feeling affirmed. Others come with a problem, wait for instructions, and leave with your solution. A third type of employee comes when called, waits for you to describe the problem, and then asks what you want them to do. Each type offers a different relationship and you respond accordingly – relational leadership in action? Not entirely. You may be giving them what they need, but without respect to who you are and your relational needs.

Different people require different types of relational interactions, but these requests should not be met at the expense of the other party. With all good intentions, you may become a victim of the people you are leading – responding to their needs without regard to your own identity. This is a relationship, but one that is out of balance, does not leverage your leadership contribution, and may leave you, the leader, drained and maybe angry and frustrated when others do not live up to your performance expectations.

Before introducing leadership practices for handling individual situations, let's step back and get personally connected using the three relational perspectives. Unless a leader knows who she is and where she stands, she

Everyone wants a piece of me – but what's left for Me Inc?

will have a struggle trying to connect others to the organization's vision. Unless you know what you bring to the game (*identity*) and how your passion (*purpose*) is excited by the organization's vision, it is hard to lead others to find their purposeful connection to that vision. How can others know they want to go where you are leading, how can they recognize the path even, unless first, you know *you* want to go there?

The beginning of a leader's transformation to a relational methodology is to first achieve clarity of personal perspective, to make the connection of his or her **Purpose** with that of the enterprise. How is the work of leading the enterprise connected with his or her passion(s) in life? What possibilities does the enterprise's vision hold for the leader? Making this connection to the vision of the enterprise (and regularly confirming its validity) is just as important for leadership as it is for each stakeholder.

The second issue for a relational leader is **Identity**, knowing the core of his or her personal Me Inc. What are the elements that define the Me Inc. in this key role, especially as regards contributions? Understanding what special attributes a leader brings to the enterprise is critical. Being able to "show up" as a person who understands who they are and what they bring to the enterprise produces genuine humility – a powerful relational tool.

The third action is to establish a personal **Accountability** system. Personal leadership accountability is measured by more than your firm's performance. On the other hand, personal leadership accountability is not about trying to "take care" of others or looking back with guilt at what we might have done better. A personal accountability system is a reflective process in real time, placing your goals, possibilities, and commitments ahead of looking good in the moment or in the past.

Purpose is in our Possibilities

We all have a mental model, a construct, a way of thinking about life, ourselves, other people, and situations. We are shaped by these thoughts and our interpretation of them. These thoughts shape the possibilities we envisage, and these thoughts filter what we see, how we hear and how we speak. They frame our relational interactions.

- What is life as a possibility – a journey, a test, a race, an adventure, a dream, a party, or simply a struggle?

- What are you as a possibility for others – a contribution, a challenge, a caretaker, or maybe a source of reflection?

- What is work as a possibility – a social connection, a creative expression, an income source, a place to live your purpose?

Life as a Possibility

How do you see life as a possibility? We are not asking you to find an answer to the meaning of life, but rather, to identify your metaphor for life. Possibilities about life are linked to this metaphor; possibilities provide the source of our passion and thus our creative energy.

- If life is a journey, you may value new experiences more than someone who sees life as a test, with pass/fail consequences resulting from each new experience.

- Life as a journey may give you a passion for adventure, a hunger to explore new ideas or new fields of knowledge. Does your life as a journey have a destination – the achievement of perfect knowledge or a passion for learning?

- You may see your existence as a relational journey, and hence, your passion in life may be meeting and getting to know (exploring) new and different people.

- If life is a race, you may have a passion for competition or be easily annoyed at those who block your path.

No one possibility is the right leadership outlook, but the point here is that there are many possible perspectives from which a leader might view the world and from which her passions spring. The point is that the connection, between this passion and the enterprise's vision, will make the difference in *where-you-are-coming-from* when taking leadership actions. When connected to a performance vision of enterprise growth, a passion for learning will express itself differently than will a passion for new experiences.

You as a Possibility

Relational interactions start with the possibility you see for yourself in each situation.

- You may be a possibility to show the way – creating a show of strength and direction.

- You may be a possibility to help others succeed – creating a supportive space for them to work.

- You may be a possibility to win – creating a competitive atmosphere.

- You may be a possibility to learn – creating space to explore new ideas.

- You may be a possibility to teach – creating a space for others to see new ways of working.

Another way to understand yourself as a possibility in each situation is to consider your commitment to each specific relational interaction. For many of us, the first commitment that surfaces is often a commitment to looking good – translate that as a possibility to be right, knowing the answer, etc. This response can create a show of strength, or it can create an atmosphere of competition – depending on the other person's possibility. It is often helpful to take a few moments and recite your commitment to create the best space to realize your objective for each interaction. For example, "I am a person committed to allowing others to see opportunity in this conversation." This makes you a possible contribution for the person with whom you are speaking, reduces right/wrong competitive positioning, and gives that person space to hear what you have to say.

The importance of understanding who you are as a commitment will be clearer if we look at an example. Let us look at how your commitment in the moment impacts both your listening and speaking mode and thus show how it impacts interactions with others.

Commitment	Listening	Speaking
To be right	For confirmation	From right opinions
To be admired	For acknowledgement	About yourself
To be finished	For distraction	With finality
To be important	To yourself	As a judge
To be heard	For an opening	Too much
To be clever	For an opportunity	In a vacuum
To be liked	For dissent	In agreement

Work as a Possibility

Work is also a possibility, and it must be a possibility to engage your passion or you will find yourself constantly drained of energy. You will wake in the morning envisioning the day ahead as merely work, something to get through because you must. If work coincides with your passion, it can be a place to live and grow. Sure, there will always be some part of our work that is less than exciting – who likes doing all of those month-end forms? But if you want to bring your real self to the job, the work must present a possibility that ignites some passion within you.

Work may be a possibility to learn – giving you energy to undertake new challenges. Work may be a possibility to win – giving you energy to exceed goals. Work may be a possibility to create – giving you energy to find unique solutions. Work may be a possibility to help – giving you energy to support others. Work may be a number of things, but unless it is a possibility that connects with a passion, it will be just a job.

Think about your passions. How do they relate to the enterprise? How do they connect with the mission of the enterprise? What part of your work activity set do you find most energizing? Do you get energized guiding others to greater clarity? Do you get energy from discovering a solution yourself or with others? Does it give you more energy to listen to others or to speak to them? All of the foregoing are interesting questions to ponder as you look for your definition of work as a possibility.

Identity makes us Real

Once you understand how your possibilities shape your perspective, the next step is to understand and respect your contribution so that authenticity emerges. Leadership techniques and tools only go so far when building relationships. Behind the words must be an authentic leader whose thoughts and actions are in sync with his or her heart. *Who you are matters; for you, the people around you, and your organization.*

The distinct individuality of a leader is defined in his or her Me Inc. description – his or her business *Identity* statement. What do you have to give in support of the performance vision? What are the contributions that define the "unique you"? Understanding what special attributes you bring to the enterprise is critical. *Knowing how you "show up" and then being responsible for the impact of this "presence" may be the single most important element of leadership.*

Why is awareness of your contribution important? You cannot be responsible for a way of being that you do not acknowledge. You cannot give what you do not own. Relationship building must have a foundation – the relationship of a leader with his or her staff within the context of the enterprise is built on a foundation of the individual leader's talents. Obviously, you must know these talents to build upon them. To describe your identity in the form of contribution is to know those gifts you have to offer to the enterprise that employs you and to society.

The best place to start the process is to do an assets and liabilities inventory. Focus first on the asset side of this balance sheet. Look at the strengths that are you. As you record each asset, ask yourself one question: "How and when might excessive use of this asset become a liability?" Write this potential liability in the second column.

Few of our liabilities are freestanding – they most often arise as the flipside of a particular strength. Seen from this strength perspective, they are easier to understand as liabilities. And seeing liabilities as the other edge of our strength sword gives us energy to work with them, whereas trying to ignore, repress, or change them can merely be exhausting.

Personal Inventory

Leadership Assets	Potential Liabilities
• I grasp situations quickly	• I may not often let others complete
• I am creative & love new challenges	• I often miss that finishing touch
• I am a great conceptualizer	• I have limited attention for detail
• I am quick to find solutions	• I can shut out other's ideas
• I use a very inclusive approach	• I can be slow to make decisions
• I allow others "space"	• I do not always provide clear direction
• I instinctively trust others	• I sometimes do not check the facts
• I accept complete responsibility	• I make decisions for others, thus allowing them to avoid responsibility

Clarity of identity is a source of measured confidence, which is to say, adult confidence: no adolescent posturing allowed. Full knowledge of self can bring about a healthy self-effacement, which is the basis of honest humility. The greater our understanding of our contribution, the more confident we are of acceptance, and thus there is no need for shows of power or other trappings of leadership under the old paradigm. This knowledge transforms one of life's greatest fears – to be discovered for who we really are – into a gift of knowing what we contribute and how and why we are connected to our world. Our sense of purpose becomes who we are, and we lead from that position of measured confidence.

What do you bring – your contribution – that is the foundation of your relationship with the organization? If you are at all unclear about your special contributions (and you do have them), start a search for the authentic you. Experience a reflecting mirror[1] process by asking friends, colleagues, your boss, and even your mate. You might even ask your mother – although she may be slightly biased. You might also start a journal or hire a coach, but by all means, do work on your own Me Inc. Personal identity is one of life's Holy Grails, and the journey to find it should be fun rather than arduous.

Let us be clear, this attempt to define Me Inc. is *not* about trying to be something you aren't or acting out a role. People do grow and thus expand their Me Inc., but each new level of growth contains within it the previous Me Inc., even though some form of transformation occurs. Thinking differently will lead to different action, and the mind can lead the heart into new truths. For example, a new "worldview" will redefine truths developed within more "localized" thinking, but our anchors are still very much intact. Knowing who you are as a leader is about maintaining an authentic understanding of yourself in relationship to the enterprise and the stakeholders involved.

Accountability keeps us Grounded

Connecting *Purpose* and *Identity* with your enterprise's performance vision is a powerful experience and a powerful tool, but no relationship is balanced unless *Accountability* is also present. In your relationship with the enterprise, what will you be accountable for – beyond the success of the firm? How should your contribution be measured? What relational standards will you hold yourself responsible to uphold? In short, what does your personal scoreboard look like?

Accountability starts by taking responsibility for how you show up – the impact of your presence. Being responsible – being accountable – for the impact of one's presence is *not* taking a "like it or lump it" attitude about your style. Nor is being responsible the often practiced art of suppressing or hiding traits that we feel are non-constructive. Being responsible *is* being authentic, or more specifically, being authentic while being conscientious of, and holding yourself accountable for, the impact of your presence with others.

> We coached a very "go to" type executive in a medium-sized enterprise. He had the ability to quickly grasp issues and find ways to handle them. If you had a problem, he had a solution. He was enthusiastic and willing to take personal risks to deliver performance. In any meeting, he had a strong personal presence that could not be denied: stiff body, unblinking eye contact, and forceful speech pattern, all behind a fixed smile. This presence led to reduced contribution from his team as he could quickly intimidate others with this forceful demeanor and quick ability to see solutions. He spoke of genuinely wanting the contribution of others, yet he ended discussions with a

quick word and/or single look. When he tried to downplay this presence with silence, his body language spoke volumes. When he tried not looking at others, he gave the impression of being bored.

We worked with him to develop an accountability scoreboard. He began to measure the number of times that solutions came from others – which was not often. He declared his accountability for this presence by giving others permission to "call his game" of intimidation and by working to define others as possibilities for learning rather than possibilities for him to be right. The immediate benefit of this accountability was a staff that responded to his honesty. They increased their responsibility for performance rather than acting to please him. Solutions started coming from others, and the group's performance improved markedly. As performance improved, this leader was able to focus on understanding his contribution (the ability to bring clarity to issues), and his need to "control the show" diminished further.

Again, we strongly suggest that you set up your own accountability scoreboard and implement a system for reviewing it or receiving feedback against your own measures of leadership performance. We are *not* suggesting 360-degree feedback against some measure of what great leaders should be. Admittedly, 360-degree feedback can be somewhat useful, but only when the process is designed to look at your identity and accountability and does not result in being merely the reflected identity of others through an evaluation of you. What we are suggesting is a process to regularly look at your performance within your identity development, feedback against your own described measures for how you wish to impact others. The question to be answered is: "How will you call yourself to account for your relationship with your people and the enterprise's performance vision?"

Note

1. *A mirror in this regard is a reflection tool designed by James R Ewing of Executive Arts, Inc. Although to the casual observer it looks like a 360 degree feedback system, it is actually a unique method of using your observations of others to understand yourself and to validate how you are perceived by others, your presence.*

Revealing Me Inc. Actions

A key to relational leadership is knowledge of who you are as a leader: Who you are considering all three elements – *purpose*, *identity*, and *accountability*. These three elements fully define your Me Inc. We end this chapter with three actions for revealing your Me Inc. You can find more details about how to complete each action at our web site: *www.ThePerformanceConnection.org*

1. Notice what others look for from you. Keep a diary of what others say, or don't say, about your contribution. If you cannot discern what they look for in each interaction, ask!

2. Complete a structured reflective process that requires you to evaluate behavioral attributes of others as well as your own.

3. Write a purpose statement for your life.

Chapter 2

"*Leadership is the art of getting someone else to do something you want done because he wants to do it.*"
Dwight D. Eisenhower

Then It's All About Them

Thoughts *matter.* Thoughts determine outcomes because thoughts inflect actions. To prove these assertions, you need only ask yourself why you are reading this book. If you are reading *The Performance Connection* with the hope of finding insights, you have defined this book as a possibility for learning. If you are reading this book to confirm that you already know how to motivate people to perform, you have defined this book as a possibility to confirm your theories. Your definition of this book will filter every phrase you read and will determine what you get out of reading it.

Thoughts about people matter even more. Thoughts about others determine our interactions and relationships with them. People respond to how we interact with them. They become for us the possibilities we define them as. In this chapter, you will look at staff members from the three relational perspectives: as *Possibilities*, as *Unique Beings*, and as *Accountable*.

Possibilities align Interactions

Why do we find it easy to take advice from some people and so hard to listen to that same advice from someone else? What pops into your mind when certain people walk into your office or call you on the phone?

Almost without exception, every person represents a distinct possibility to us, a possibility that is in turn realized as we interact with that person. If the person is viewed as an expert, we listen to that person in order to learn from them. If a person is viewed as less than competent (or as lower on the organizational totem pole), we listen in order to correct or refute what they say – this person represents a possibility for us to be right or superior. If a person is viewed as a true colleague, we listen for the sake of interaction and dialogue. Once again: Possibilities Align Actions and Interactions.

> *A possibility is definable as something believed or seen as reachable or likely, a deeply felt belief or trust, often unspoken but felt, that a specific outcome may happen or can occur. A possibility is not to be mistaken for a wish or a fantasy, however. A possibility is a view of a situation that is "felt" to be realizable. In story terms, a possibility is energy – an energy created by verbal or mental narratives of glorious or fateful deeds.*
>
> *A possibility is not an expectation of certainty either, however. That is, a possibility does not fail, it just fails to materialize. Thus the failed materialization of a possibility simply gives rise to another possibility. On the other hand, a failed expectation of certainty gives rise to disappointment – and often anger. Where an expectation of certainty has been "banked" emotionally, a true possibility remains as something yet to be realized. A lost or failed possibility just opens the door for the creation of another possibility.*

Although how we define other people is a choice, our initial reaction about someone often occurs for us as a truth that does not feel much like a choice. In reality, this reaction is just a story about your history with that person. This is not a universal truth, but *your* truth – others may have an entirely different truth about the individual in question. Stay with us on this one. The first step in making a choice as regards the possibility a person represents is to first acknowledge the current possibility they represent for you, your current truth or opinion of them. Then, you take the important step of consciously choosing a new possibility for the person – you create a new truth.

Here is the kicker: you must teach yourself to believe your declaration. One process that allows you to do that sounds a bit unusual, but it works. This process stems from the observation that we internalize (listen to ourselves talk) the words we speak as well as the thoughts we create. Perhaps more importantly, we subconsciously believe what we say to ourselves, and why wouldn't we? If we cannot believe ourselves, who can we believe? The more often we speak something, the more we believe it. So, watch what stories you tell, for they just might become your "truths." Or, you can make this fact work for you with others: You can create a new story about them.

To create this new story, start by stating a new possibility for the person. Let's say the person is Susan Black, and for you, she is currently defined as a complaint. Every time she comes into your office, all you hear is a complaint about something or someone else in the office. Now, write out a sentence in this form. "In the matter of Susan Black: she is a person committed to improving performance standards in the office." Every day for the next seven days, stand in front of a mirror and repeat the statement aloud.

By day five, you will be feeling the truth of the statement, and Susan will begin to emerge as an opportunity to improve the performance standards of the office. By day seven, all you will hear from Susan is performance improvement opportunities. Heard as an opportunity rather than a complaint, Susan *will* become a new possibility, and both you and she *will* respond to this new possibility.

Though this may seem outrageous and unlikely to be effective, it is a proven strategy. Susan has been defined as a complainer, which is your truth. *We are suggesting that you can redefine your truth about any person.* After all, wasn't the original truth about Susan created in much the same manner? By accepting an historical, emotional, reaction to Susan, this emotional truth became a reality. This same process can create a new truth about Susan – as a person committed to improving performance standards.

This concept of people as possibilities has major implications for leading an enterprise. Psychologists have recognized for years that behavior and actions are motivated by attitude, and the simple concept that *attitude is shaped by the possibilities we create* is critical to relational leadership. When we see positive possibilities in others, we acknowledge their potential.

This "seeing" people as performance possibilities causes a leader to look for what people might contribute rather than where they might fail. When people are seen as performance possibilities, we look for their positive attributes and their contribution when engaging in interactions.

Take a few minutes to think about some people you deal with on a regular basis. Using this language of possibilities, how do you define them? What kind of connection exists between this definition and your relationship with them? For a leader, the following might occur:

- Acting from a possibility that people are not competent, leaders will withhold delegating authority, require everything to be "passed by them," and ensure that detailed reviews occur before approval to proceed is given.

- Acting from a possibility that employees are lazy, leaders will give more directives and insist on regular progress checks and status reports.

- Acting from a possibility that people want to learn, grow, exceed expectations and do well, leaders will ask for lofty performance goals and give people freedom to find ways to reach them.

Uniqueness is their Strength

Each person is unique. Their talents are individual. The ability to see the uniqueness of the individual is an important relational leadership skill – Contribution Defines Relationships. This understanding of individual uniqueness is also critical for the individual as they develop their Me Inc.

Respecting individual uniqueness is not about letting someone talk about themselves during the coffee break. Respecting uniqueness is an authentic desire to know them and to help them know themselves better. It is the ability to see and relate to the individual from their contribution perspective, matching that contribution with the needs of the business, and reflecting for them their gifts of contribution. Contribution values the person for who they are as well as what activities they perform.

The truth is, everyone wants to understand themselves better, especially in the area of contribution. Thus, one of the greatest gifts you can give another person is the gift of understanding their special talents or

That identity fits you perfectly madam!

contribution – the gift of *identity*. As you work with them to better the business, be a mirror for them to work on their Me Inc. Listen and watch for their contributions, reflect the potential you hear, and use this observation as the basis of your possibility for them.

When looking for the unique person, begin with their positive attributes. We seem trained to look first for what is wrong with a person. This negative aspect is not the uniqueness we most appreciate – nor does it do us the most good.

> *We recall an interview process that was designed to iden-*
> *tify the flaws of the individual candidate – or at least that's*
> *the way the process was set up. The team interviewing the*
> *candidate was required to look for "compelling reasons why*
> *this person should not be appointed?" Then, having spent*

hours interviewing to discover a "fatal flaw" as the basis to reject candidates, the successful candidate, presumably the one without a fatal flaw (just run of the mill flaws), was invited to lead the organization. The process somehow seemed backward. How would you feel about joining a team after such an introduction, one that revolved around the negative identification of your Me Inc.?

Find something you admire and can use to further the objectives of the enterprise about each person and make it the center of your conversations with each. If you're worried that always looking for the positive will perpetuate existing weaknesses (something we all have), be assured, it will not. As noted previously, performance weaknesses are most often the flipside of a particular strength. This double-edged sword effect will show itself as the conversation expands around the development of these strengths. When a weakness can be seen from its strength perspective, we have a foundation for growth rather than the threat of failure to propel how we deal with this issue.

We have a colleague who is brilliant at finding new ways to help individuals and teams find empowerment – defined here as the willingness to take action and be responsible in the face of opposition. He can work this magic during the course of a conversation, and he can design a process to make it happen – seldom the same process but a new twist. If you have a new idea, he is all ears and right into the conversation. But guess what? Don't ask him to ever follow up. His passion for new and creative ways to enable people to grow does not extend beyond getting them moving. Once they are two steps down the path, he is on to a new challenge. He is not a finisher – the other side of his passionate, creative sword is the dull edge of not finishing and following-up.

Do we start conversations with this colleague about why he doesn't work on this obvious weakness? Not if we want his brilliance – a possibility to engage people in improving performance. We relate to him from this contribution, and we design work processes that avoid reliance on his dull edge. He is a unique and wonderful person to work with, and we appreciate his special abilities. We can also talk about the other edge, here with you or with him over coffee, without threatening his identity or challenging his Me Inc.

Scoring and assessment systems that simply compare individuals against a standard list of competencies or behaviors, and then focus training on weaknesses, are only half complete. Without understanding how these missing attributes are linked to the uniqueness of the individual, these systems fail to access a powerful link to learning – our passion-driven strengths. Everyone has a different set of strengths and competencies. Everyone also has identifiable downside attributes that arise from these strengths. To deny this is to deny who individuals are in an attempt to pretend everyone is (or ought to be) the same. To then attempt training activities that ignore the true source of these downside attributes is often an attempt to force round pegs into square holes.

It follows that traditional performance appraisal systems, whereby all are measured against a standard set of norms and the majority are rated "C" or "average" or "meeting standards," is a de-motivational exercise. It is human to desire recognition of our individuality. Few, if any of us, feel good to be labeled as average, which signifies that we are *just* an accountant or *just* an engineer or etc. Interestingly, when surveyed, over 80 percent of people rate themselves as *better than average* drivers, which would seem to suggest rather pointedly that forced-ranking exercises that place 60-70 percent of the population in the "average" category may not be the best way to inspire staff. Interestingly, companies often accompany this "average" review rating with an "average" pay raise, effectively spending money to de-motivate people.

When processes that encourage the emergence of identity, rather than conspiring to suppress it, are in place, two things occur. First, individuals focus on their true gifts, on doing what they do best and what they like to do. They become more efficient as they work from a clearer perspective of the strength they bring to the team relationship. Second, as the individual gains more confidence in his or her contribution to the relationship, their need for individual acknowledgement is fulfilled without explicit credit for each and every activity they undertake.

People have both a primary need for this individual Me Inc. identity and a secondary need to be a part of something larger – Team Inc. A leader's focus on individual uniqueness or identity thru contribution is the organizational answer to the Me Inc. dilemma that has plagued organizations since the 1980s, when companies first became *unable* to keep the "lifetime-employment-in-exchange-for-loyalty" contract. As identity becomes the definer for Me Inc., the individual's need for self understanding is fulfilled. The individual is then available to support the something-larger driver – Team Inc. Me Inc. allows for autonomy, while Team Inc. provides a place for contribution and community.

Accountability requires Calibration

How often do people you work with ask if they are doing a good job – perhaps not that directly but at least implying the desire for some performance reinforcement? Every one of us *likes* to know that we are meeting the expectations of our job. Every one of us *needs* to know that we are meeting expectations in our relationships. *Competition Sets the Standards,* but without some method of connection to the organization's performance goal and calibration of the contribution, perception and reality quickly become distant relatives. A relational leader ensures that accountability, responsibility, and objective calibration are ever present as a part of the business process.

> We were engaged to coach a business team experiencing difficulties initiating business improvement changes. In a business environment of constantly changing priorities, the senior team needed staff to provide fit-for-purpose solutions and to respond with flexibility as performance demands changed. Instead, most change requirements resulted in requests for more specific policies or direction from the top. The organization used a management-by-objective process against detailed work plans, and was constantly faced with prioritization problems and lack of progress when the plans required adaptation to changing circumstances – something that was happening with increasing frequency. Not surprisingly, staffs' number one complaint was about lack of communication from the leadership.

> However, what staff called a lack of communication was really a lack of calibration. Because performance demands were subject to change, management resisted establishing clear outcome-based accountability measures, and the organization had nothing to guide decisions and no way to calibrate their performance – they were measured against activity-based plans and the plans always changed. The solution was to introduce clear, measurable, business goals instead of work plans to guide the organization. As soon as these were clarified for the organization, individuals were

> *able to understand the criteria for decisions and were able to feel connected to the performance demands of the business. Communication is important, but not as important as having clarity about the performance goals against which the organization must calibrate itself.*

Leading staff members into the world of accountability is not just about a performance measurement process, setting objectives and measuring results – although these latter two are very important. As the third leg of the relational-needs stool, the accountability perspective includes relational responsibility in addition to results achievement.

The Matter of Responsibility

Accountability as a relational attribute is an attitude of responsibility – seeing how our actions, attitudes, and choices impact the outcomes with which we must live. Acceptance of how others react to our choices without the need to justify those choices or to argue that others are not being fair is the sign of a responsible person.

Accountability as a relational attribute is *not* the use of competition in relationships. Competition is a biological law of nature – it sets the standards of performance required to ensure survival. However, competition (like winning at another's expense) is not healthy in a relationship or a relational model of leadership. Competition as a win/lose paradigm allows individuals to act without taking responsibility for the impact of their actions on others, and competition allows independence and not interdependence to flourish within the organization.

Far too often, we hear leaders say, "A little competition is a good thing, for it brings out the best in people." Then they establish subtle and not so subtle competition *within* their organizations. Then, in the face of a strategy of integrated services, they inevitably complain about lack of cooperation between business teams. We believe that anything beyond "friendly" internal competition is *never, never* good from an overall organizational perspective – internal competition reinforces a world of independence and will work to make organizations and individuals less, not more, responsible.

In order to establish the concept of true responsibility in an organization, accountable leaders take responsibility for the impacts of their own decisions and hold others accountable for theirs, keeping relational responsibility in balance. They avoid the tendency to be the parent-as-leader who makes all decisions for others, effectively removing them from responsibility for their own failures or successes. And they refuse to allow staff members to assume the victim's position, blaming others as the cause of all problems or negative outcomes in their life.

The Matter of Relativity

Because *Competition Sets the Standards,* performance accountability is a relative concept. Whether you are measuring performance in terms of profit, behavior, unit cost, rate of return on investment, service delivery standards, etc., the level of performance required is a moving target. True, customers and other stakeholders often make definable demands for performance, but the level of performance they demand relates to their alternative choices – your competition. To be best-in-class, you must accept that performance expectations are constantly changing. Historical benchmarking does not show the whole picture – it is a motionless picture of a moving vehicle and therefore misleading. Worse yet, it is a picture taken yesterday.

> *We often repeat the story about a manufacturer in the 1980's, when benchmarking was first in vogue. They did a benchmarking exercise and discovered that their productivity was about 20% under that of a leading competitor. Management promptly set a three-year goal to improve productivity by 6% per year. If they reached this goal each year, they reasoned, they would catch the leading manufacturer by the end of the third year – a fair target for the organization! The business not only reached the goal but surpassed it, actually delivering over 7% in annual productivity improvements. Realizing they had beaten their targets, the leadership judged the effort a success, paid bonuses, and celebrated the victory.*
>
> *Then one of their engineers revisited the leading competitor. What the engineer found was devastating! The leading competitor had set 8% goals, made 11%, and was further ahead than before. Not only did this present sales and pricing problems, it presented an organizational management problem. While management had judged the organization's performance a success by using "the boss sets the performance targets" rule, the Competition Sets the Standards law determined that the result was actually a bust.*

How did the staff react? "Management told us to improve by 6%, we actually delivered 7%, and now they tell us we failed? What kind of crap is this? This is all just a game to get us to work harder! I told you they could not be trusted – this just proves it to me!"

The use of a good accountability process – setting and making goals explicit – ended up in disappointment and mistrust of management. Why? Because the organization did not understand that competitive performance is a relative term and that competition is the ultimate judge of success or failure. Instead, the organization was led to believe that its performance standards could be artificially set, and success judged, by the organization's hierarchical leadership.

In truth, all specific performance criteria are moving targets. True, they must be fixed as goals to make them tangible and real, but the competition is always raising the bar, and so we know that whatever targets we establish today, tomorrow's targets will be higher. Your organization might hit the target where it has been set by the leadership and not be successful because the competition might have raised the bar higher than you anticipated, as in our example. Of course, the opposite is also true – you might miss the target and be successful competitively because the competition moved slower or was less able to adapt to changes in the environment. Thus your enterprise must remain light on its feet, so to speak, and be willing to revise performance objectives as the overall picture, as viewed in real time, demands.

The Matter of Transparency

Competitive standards may be a moving target, but the basis for individual and collective accountability must be clear. "We will tell you later if you hit the target" is unacceptable, and a strategy for disaster. Success or failure cannot be left simply to the judgment of the boss in an after-the-fact evaluation process. Individuals and teams need to clearly understand the basis of performance expectations, which will enable them to move out of the parent/child model of working to please others. The transparency of process and targets increases responsibility and expands creativity, and success or failure is then understood as an outcome of competitive performance rather than the judgment of a superior.

Because leaders often have the breadth of vision (and the information) that allows them to clarify the performance standards needed to stay in the game, it is easy for a leader to get swept into the position of target setter, and by default, to become the judge of performance. When a leader sits in judgment, a dependency relationship exists between the parties. Cooperation, mutuality, reciprocity or partnership concepts are not available to the parties in this situation, and leaders are not free to coach and support as long as they serve as watchman and judge. The relationship as well as opportunities for further performance improvement

He may be guilty – but does he need to feel guilty?

is limited. Experience tells us that working to please others is a recipe for mediocrity, not excellence – the consequence of such a relationship is a trying-to-look-good mentality.

Leaders determine *what* standards or areas of measurement are relevant to ensure strategic alignment, but once again, leadership does not set the level of the standards – competition does. Once the strategic context for the metric has been communicated, a relational leader requires the team to establish and justify the competitive logic of the targets as well as to request (and justify) the resources they will require. A relational leader sets the boundaries – what staff must do as well as what they cannot do – the *values* to which they must adhere and etc. (we will say more about these boundaries when we introduce a leadership model in *Chapter 4 – Ensure Responsibility*), but then include the team in the process of goal setting so that they understand the rationale of the marketplace: why these goals make sense relative to the competition.

During the transition process, it is natural for individuals and teams to ask leadership, "What is the target you will accept?" We suggest that you take this opportunity to further the transition process by placing the responsibility with them, by turning the question around: "What is the target *you* will set to meet competitive pressures?" When your team(s) begins a negotiation process for target setting, you can be fairly sure they still do not understand the transparency issue and see you as the setter of standards and the judge of their success, but as noted, this is also an opportunity to help them in this regard. This simple strategy is a gentle push towards enacting transparency.

These first two chapters focused on identifying your Me Inc. and then asked you to define the possibilities you see in others. Now we are ready to apply the knowledge gained from personal reflection and individual relational understandings to the organizational context. Each of the next four chapters explains a key leadership practice that is essential to the development of a *Perform and Learn* culture.

Actions for Understanding Others

The definitions we hold of others are so powerful that they control our relationships, but these definitions are sometimes hidden from us. Here are three actions that may help you understand who others are for you and how these definitions impact your relationship with your key stakeholders. Again, you can find more detail about each of these action items and discover other relational management processes and tools by going to the web site: *www.ThePerformanceConnection.org*

1. Make a list of each of your key stakeholders. For each person, write a short paragraph describing what they contribute to your relationship. Ask yourself, "How does this contribution support my performance commitments?"

2. Define your commitment to each stakeholder. For each of these key stakeholders, write a commitment statement, such as, "In regard to Susan Black: I am committed to helping her appreciate the strength of her contribution."

3. Listen to the language you use with various stakeholders. For a 30-day period, keep a daily record of the one-on-one conversations with specific stakeholders. Note the words you used and the responses these words generated. In particular, notice how often you find yourself standing in judgment or making decisions for others based upon your determination of what is best for them.

Chapter 3

"The value of an idea lies in the using it."
Thomas Edison

From End to Start

Leadership always begins with Purpose – being able to articulate where the enterprise is going and how each activity supports this direction. This is easy to say and far less easy to do; and even once you are familiar with the concept, it is often easy to slip out of the habit and to forget the power of this practice to guide everyday actions. Practicing *From End to Start* brings clarity to outcomes and provides focus. It allows you to move from clarity regarding the overall vision to clarity regarding everyday tasks, like managing meetings and conversations, and much more in between. This practice also underscores the need to be clear about the realities of today's starting point as activities move through time. Although this sounds like common sense, when we look at many of our current routines, it is amazing how often we are unclear about our desired outcomes or how often we try to make past decisions look right – effectively working toward an old beginning instead of toward our desired end goals.

The purpose of this chapter is to explain how this practice of moving *From End to Start* applies to key leadership activities.

Our Two Anchors

We call the habit of speaking of the future with no apparent connection to the present *"dream leadership."* We call speaking only of the present with no apparent connection to the future *"blind leadership."* Being anchored in a vision for the future evokes possibility and purpose, and being anchored in the present demands accountability, and both perspectives are necessary. Thus relational leaders need to provide both anchors for their organizations. In short, leaders and their organizations need to be:

- Grounded by the reality of today – the **Start**

- Propelled by a vision of the future – the **End**.

Admittedly, the tension between the pull of the future and the anchor in the present will create some anxiety and perhaps cause some discomfort for the leader and the organization, but that tension can also create energy for action.

Be careful what that action is, however. All too often, a leader's response to this organizational anxiety is what we refer to as the *"Parent Trap."* Perhaps you have seen this happen. The CEO tells the employees of the organization a story about where the enterprise needs to be in the future. Everyone is figuratively holding their breath, waiting to be told how this new future will happen. Then the CEO outlines the solution. The organization breathes a collective sigh of relief, for the leader-as-parent has come to their rescue. The employees of the organization are off the hook as regards a successful implementation. If this new future does not come about, it will be the CEO's plan that failed and not the employees.

The leader's role is to engage their organization in this future rather than to merely outline its parameters or to map the route. This requires a guided discussion that allows others to see this new future as a possibility. When holding such a discussion, rather than "having the answers," be open and honest. Try the following approach:

- Acknowledge the tension. It exists and you are aware of its presence.

- Be authentic in your discussions of the present situation. Let people voice their concerns and fears – acknowledge these concerns.

- Then ask, "In the face of these fears, what might we expect to see people doing?"

- Now encourage a frank discussion of the opportunities presented by the future vision and goals.

- Move the discussion to things that must change in order to reach the described future. What stands in the way of the new vision of tomorrow? What would they need to do to overcome these barriers?

- Then ask each person to write one action that leadership should take and one action that leadership should stop doing in order to achieve this new vision of the future. Also ask them to write down two things they could do as individuals and two things they could stop doing. This strategy short-circuits the tendency to expect leadership to do everything and to generate more actions for busy people during times of change. Collect the leadership actions, which will be useful feedback, but please do not promise to act on these. A promise to act will be viewed as merely an extension of the parent-child relationship, whereby the leader takes responsibility for change and staff abdicates.

- Now, ask people what first step actions they might take in moving toward the goals previously outlined.

This process lets people get real about the current situation. It allows them to describe their own possibilities for the future. They get a chance to say what they think others need to do, but most importantly, they get to see what *they* need to do and what first steps *they* need to take.

As this picture of the future as a possibility begins to take shape, you can accelerate their actions by getting them to describe this new future in their words and then list the actions they must take to realize this future possibility. We labeled a tool for implementing this practice a "Merlin," as in Merlin the Magician.

As the story goes, Merlin could predict the future and was thus able to assist King Arthur. However, Merlin had a trick. He imagined he was already in the future and what the outcome was. He then worked out what steps had to be taken to achieve this future, essentially starting at the end of the story and working backwards. He worked out who had to do what to achieve this outcome, and then he advised Arthur on the first steps to take. Here we have it in an ancient context and succinctly modeled for you – the practice of moving *From End to Start*.

To implement a "Merlin" we ask a person, or several of persons, to imagine themselves at a particular time in the future (in this case, post-implementation to meet some challenge in the present) and to describe what the world looks like as a result of having successfully met whatever the challenge on which they are working. As an aside, you will find that people have varying abilities to stand at different points in the future. Some are able to stand no more than a year out, and fewer will be able to stand 5 years out – and very few can comfortably stand 10 years or more out. Next, you ask them to describe the last step that they did or the last thing that happened before the desired outcome was delivered. Then the step or event previous to this one and so on. In sequential steps, we move them from the future back to the present. When the imaginary journey is completed, they will have the end vision and have built an action plan for getting there from the start position, from the present. Finally, ask the participants what others involved in the process did in their imagined trip through time in order to accomplish this vision of the future. Do not make this portion of the process linear, but rather, make it an organic retrospective process. Together, they will begin to describe a tangible vision of successful delivery of this envisaged future, and at the same time, they will be able to acknowledge others' unique contribution to achieving this future.

A Fresh Start

Have you noticed how many leaders make their greatest contribution during their first year on the job? They arrive at a new job having no relationship to past decisions, and thus they are not trying to make past decisions right. They *Start* the new job with their own *End* in view. For them, the past is a story that they do not want or need to hear, and they make fresh choices without feeling guilty if they are changing a process or outcome that resulted from somebody else's past decision. Yet, once they have been on the job a while, they seem to get bogged down. Why is that? Is it because their *Start* point stays fixed? Over time, they begin to take actions designed to make the decisions they took at their *Start* look right, even as the world changes. In effect, leaders get hooked by the past and are holding on to a *Start* position that is now history.

This tendency is most obvious when it comes to project investment – decisions get made with an eye to sunk costs rather than based on money-forward considerations. The emotional attachment to making the original investment decision look correct pulls the organization into wasteful future investments, even when it is obvious to the neutral observer that a better solution is available, either due to technology advances or market changes. But this legacy concept also occurs in regard to simpler issues. We have seen meetings that were established for one situation perpetuate themselves after the situation has been resolved. We have seen reports that were requested for a singular purpose continued because they were once useful. We have seen organizational structure or positions that were established for a particular purpose continued because "we have always had this position."

> *As an example, at one point in our own history, we made the decision to open an office in a new location. We had developed a new client there, had older clients in this location that we serviced from a different office, and there were potentially other clients in the area. Shortly before finalizing the lease on the office, after a great deal of searching before we located a great office, the new client reorganized and our workload was reduced dramatically as a result. It became clear that growth in that market had slowed. Nevertheless, we went ahead and signed the lease – deciding that we would make what was a good decision at the time be right in hindsight! The nagging doubt in the back of our minds was the voice to which we should have been listening. We never did make that decision right, and the move was a costly mistake. We had set a goal based not on today but on a past decision. Had we allowed ourselves to start afresh, we would have realized, first, that the original decision had been a good one, but second, that the forces acting on our business had changed and that no amount of dreaming about possibilities was going to change this fact. It should have been the time for a different action.*

In today's rapid-pace business environment, we often receive new information that could provide a new context for yesterday's decisions. The object lesson is quite clear: Learn from your past but do not get hooked by it. Do not get trapped into working toward making yesterday's decisions look correct, when in reality, a change is needed. Arrive each day to an awareness of where your organization stands within its environment – keep the *Start* new each day. For a tenured leader, practicing the art of starting fresh each day provides a better condition than it does for a new appointee. A leader with knowledge of the past can arrive informed by yesterday's learning, starting from a clear understanding of the environment today, and be guided by a dynamic vision for tomorrow.

This is not an excuse to be a wishy-washy leader who has no anchor in the future and changes his or her mind like a random number generator. This is not about being a good politician and trying to please the stakeholder's present at the moment. Practicing the art of a new *Start* each day is about being authentic in your commitment to a future but not blinded by the all too human tendency to defend past decisions. It is a brave leader who is willing to say, "Knowing what I know today, I am going to change yesterday's decision." It is a *perform-and-learn* leader who is willing to recognize the need for a fresh *Start* and then to make one.

Face the Future

From End to Start keeps an organization focused on the direction it is going rather than on looking backwards. Performance goals are in the future. In order to be pulled toward them, the organization needs to be pointed in that direction at all times.

As a leader, it is often easy to get trapped in stories about the past, either by patiently listening to explanations of why things have not gone well or by letting people spend too much time bragging about past accomplishments. People need acknowledgement for their accomplishments, and when appropriate, they must also be aware that the situation into which they have gotten themselves is a result of their choices and actions – save the latter for a private conversation about their performance.

Sometimes the stories are invited by asking these questions: "How do we find ourselves in this situation? Who is to blame for this mess? Why did we do that?" Such an investigation is interesting, but these questions are not very valuable for a forward-looking organization. Each of these questions is backward-facing, and spending too much time looking for the answers is to move the organization backward, not forward. Here is a rule: spend 5 percent of your time explaining the situation and 95 percent of your time working on a solution.

Engaging in stories about the past is like driving a car by looking in the rearview mirror. You will keep running into barriers that impede forward progress. After you hit them, the barriers are easy to see and become the focus of the conversation – first as an excuse and then as plans for what to do about the barriers the next time they appear. Meanwhile, new barriers are on the horizon and we are not looking for them. Sometimes, these backward discussions are so intense that it is like taking your hands completely off the steering wheel and driving by adjusting the rearview mirror to get a better view of what went wrong – or in some cases what went right. If you want a better chance at getting to your end point, keep the conversation focused toward the *End*.

The year 1991 had been a great one for Dennis as a leader. By early 1992, he had the facts and figures to prove that 1991 was exceptional. Under the auspices of motivating his enterprise, he put together a slide presentation and went about showing them what a great job they had done. After several weeks of this road show, a chap stopped by his office early one morning. He popped his head in the door and said, "Dennis, I feel sorry for you!"

"Feel sorry for me!" he said. "How can that be? Don't you know that 1991 was the greatest year of my professional life!"

"Yes" he said, "I know. You are going around telling everyone about it! What I am sorry for you about is that you are a relatively young man and it must be awful sad to have to wake up for the rest of your life knowing that your best year is behind you!" With that, he left.

Dennis stood for a moment with his mouth agape. He looked around and realized that 1992 was almost one-quarter over and things were going downhill rapidly. He had been so intent on bragging about the past that the future had no chance of success. Needless to say, he turned himself to face forward and got busy connecting to the future and not the past year.

Bragging and making excuses are both stories about the past. They focus the conversation in a backward-looking direction. They are not vision-driven behaviors and seldom, if ever, serve an organization's future.

Daily Applications

From End to Start is vital for planning and managing meetings. What is the purpose of this meeting? What are the outcomes expected? Being clear about the outcomes that are expected from a meeting is a leap forward and gives context to agenda planning and meeting management.

Use this question to achieve clarity regarding basic conversations: "What do we want to get out of this discussion?" This immediately puts everyone on the same page, and if appropriate, before time has been wasted, this practice can serve to acknowledge that differences exist. This question, and the answers you receive, create clarity and focus for the discussion.

Do not send anyone off on a task without clarity about what the *End* should look like. Here are some examples of the questions that you should ask first:

- "What are the goals for that project team or taskforce?"

- "What is it you want me to hear from this conversation?" (Whenever you are unclear about where a conversation is going, ask about the *End*.)

- "What do I want to accomplish today?" (You ask this question as you approach your daily work.)

Requiring clarity about the purpose of each action and the outcomes expected to arise out of it is the single most important efficiency-generating practice for a leader. Such clarity will stop you from doing many things and will alter how you do others. After all, on the days that you prepare a "to-do" list, how much more efficient is your day? How many of the items get done in a simpler manner after you write down what you want to do? Now, add a line for the purpose of each action and list what tangible outcome you are after, and you have a tool for fulfilling this practice that will further energize your to-do list and make it even more efficient.

If you ever want to stop a conversation about a problem someone is relaying to you, ask one of these questions: "What is it you want me to hear?" or "What will you be expecting of me after I listen?" This strategy can sound abrupt, and perhaps it is for it disrupts someone's story, but it also forces clarity into their thinking and puts on the table the real purpose of the conversation. Diverting the focus of the discussion to its future purpose will either allow that purpose to be revealed much faster or clarify that there is no purpose – or no *End* in sight.

Most of us need to vent every now and then – we just need to complain. We can allow that need to manifest itself in others as long as the person makes it clear that the purpose of the conversation is to complain. "I need to vent, and I want you to hear this as just that, a complaint. I do not want a solution or for you to do anything. I just want to spend five minutes complaining about how unfair life is for me at the moment." Great, now we know how to listen to the story and how to respond. "Wow, life is really unfair. Glad you shared that with me and got it out of your system. Now, back to the future."

When you are clear about the outcomes you desire, those around you will also be able to understand your *End* – and your effectiveness and your organization's effectiveness at realizing that *End* will improve markedly. Keep *From End to Start* at the front of your mind in everything that you do.

History or Future

Many of us look at life in the same way as we look through a telescope at the stars in the sky. It feels like we are looking at the present but we are in fact looking at the distant past. Emotionally, we are still gripped by events that now lie in the past, their reverberation lies with us and consumes much of our discussion time and our emotional energies.

We are not suggesting that an understanding of historical events is not important – it is. There is much to be learned from it. There is, however, a great danger in being locked in the past – whether it be in a past success or past failure. Where the heart and head are, the hands will be there also. If exploring a past event will get you to your desired outcome, then this is time well spent. If not, well, you have a choice – yesterday's history or tomorrow's future.

In order to take an organization forward, there are only two places to be: in the "*Now,*" the arena of living, and in the future, the arena of possibility. The past is only a story, a perspective that holds us prisoner if we let it occupy our time. Practice letting the past be just that: *in* the past. Be clear about your vision for the future and connect your purpose for as many *now* actions as possible to that future. The more actions that are connected to the future, the sooner it will arrive. This is equally true about the past. The more of your time spent facing it, the more likely it is that you will find yourself there once again.

Actions for Facing the Future

It is so very easy to get hooked by our past, and thus allow the past to get recreated as our future. Following are two suggestions to help keep this from happening:

1. We suggest you undertake a simple exercise. For one week, record the amount of time you spend focused backward. Whether at work or home, keep a record of the time spent in conversation about events that are more than one day old. (This timeframe lets you ask your significant other and/or the kids about their day, or vice versa.) Ask yourself, "Besides the enjoyment of tapping some interesting emotional connections, what is the value of this time?"

2. As you begin each week, take a few moments to reflect on what you learned during the past week. Think about whether you should look anew at any past decisions in light of what you know today.

Chapter 4

You cannot escape the responsibility of tomorrow by evading it today.
Abraham Lincoln

Enable Responsibility

hy do good leaders want responsible staff, people who grasp the big picture, act without specific direction, and communicate well with others as they work? Because these leaders know they must get virtually everything done through the efforts of others. The real power for performance delivery resides with the people doing the tasks. Although good leaders have huge influence, they have little direct power over the tasks required. Most of a leader's control power is after-the-fact.

To get responsible people, we use a leadership model that reinforces individual and team responsibility while simultaneously focusing everyone on the performance demands of the business. In this chapter, we introduce this "enabling responsibility" model.

The enabling responsibility model is amazingly straightforward. There are four elements to the model[1]: **Direction**, **Boundaries**, **Space** and **Coaching/Support**.

This model is brought to life through something we call the *Performance Conversation*. The Performance Conversation is a single-themed discussion that takes place over time and at different locations. Its timeframe is the present and future – not the past – and its context is this enabling

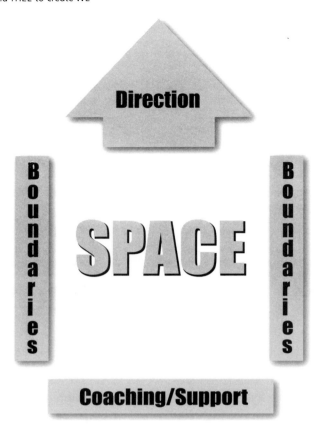

responsibility model. We will discuss a Performance Conversation after defining the elements of this model.

Direction

None of the four elements of the model is more important than the others, but the beginning place is *Direction – From End to Start.* Direction is the result of building the future in the minds of staff.

Direction refers to the objective, or where you are headed and why the goal is important. It is a case for action – why is this goal necessary? Direction is used to engage the individual (or team) in a performance commitment by finding relationships between their Purpose and the Living Vision of the organization.

Direction requires that the other party understand the goals and their context within the big picture, and thus, must be more than just a description or vague generalization. It must contain the performance standards for competitive performance. Direction involves establishing tangible goals, setting targets, and defining outcomes with enough clarity that the person or persons being directed will be able to know their progress toward meeting the goals – they must know what success will look like as they achieve it.

Boundaries

Boundaries define the freedom to act, or stated slightly differently, are the conditions of governance. These can take the form of policies for a company, limits for a task, or the use of Values to guide acceptable behaviors. Boundaries should include things to be done and things that should *not* be done. Setting boundaries involves telling, informing, advising, and getting enough feedback to be assured that the participants and the leader have a common definition of what the boundaries are. In dealing with boundaries, it is not enough to merely *tell* the employee what they are, such as merely having a policy in place and informing the employee what it is. There must be an assurance that the other party understands any boundary's application in particular situations and accepts that boundary. This acceptance needs to be explicit rather than implicit – a useful part of the process is to have these boundaries played back to you in the individual's own words or in writing.

Application of boundaries requires common sense in their application and enforcement along with the aforementioned process of assurance of understanding and acceptance on the part of the individual. When it comes to matters of governance, boundaries are prescriptive, i.e. ethical behavior means adherence to both the intent and letter of the law. However, other policy boundaries may establish a framework for decision making, wherein managers must interpret a particular boundary's exact application for each circumstance. Examples of boundaries are: limits on authority (prescriptive), deadlines, required elements of work, parties to be consulted, etc.

Boundaries are for guiding behaviors but are not for limiting performance options or restricting creativity. Boundaries set relative to the level of competency of the individual or team are more useful than hard procedural limits, but these less prescriptive boundaries require a greater level of skill to establish and manage. When setting Boundaries that enable responsibility, you might use the following guide:

- Assume individuals are competent at their jobs until they prove otherwise

- Give choices with possible consequences rather than directing a specific action

- Treat failure individually rather than collectively punishing with tighter controls

Boundaries are an opportunity to help teams and individuals learn about interdependent relationships, such as a requirement to be responsible for the impact of their actions on others. Boundaries can be requirements to obtain approval from others or to consult with others before acting. They can be requirements to let other interdependent parties set certain performance criteria that become part of the Direction element. As the Space element of the model expands, the Boundaries require greater levels of collaboration and interdependent relationships.

Space

Space is defined as the freedom to act and is a consequence of setting Direction, setting Boundaries and letting people get on with the job. Providing the right Space is the critical leadership task to enable responsibility. Space is a measure of competency, and as such, is one measure of organizational capacity. In developing an organization to higher levels of performance, greater accountability, and increased innovation, the task of leadership can be viewed as opening up the Space within which people operate.

However, to enable responsibility, leaders do not have to suddenly provide a huge amount of Space. As people learn to handle more and more responsibility, the Space within which they can operate can be developed over time. If more Space is provided than the individuals are capable of handling (they do not have the skills), they become overwhelmed. Space is a consequence of skills, knowledge, and the amount of responsibility the recipient is capable of accepting.

A leader or leadership team that does not give Space will continue managing the detail while a changing environment buffets the organization, putting in long hours to do everyone else's job less than adequately.

Coaching/Support

The key to opening up the necessary Space is *Coaching/Support*. An individual new to a task may be given very little space initially. This individual will need assistance to work more independently, and assistance can take the form of an integrated training/work plan or on-the-job teaching.

Training, when done by a third-party instructor, is not a direct element of Coaching/Support. The leader's Coaching/Support role in training is to provide the context – how the training will impact Space, Boundaries, or be linked to Direction. Without leadership involvement before and after, training programs have only a 1 in 10 chance of altering performance. After the formal training, the Coaching/Support role becomes a collaboration process to assist with the application of the new skill. Signing someone up for a training class or program is not providing Coaching/Support – this may be the necessary act of authorizing or approving as part of a control process but is not Coaching/Support.

Coaching/Support is the act of increasing an individual's capacity to take effective action. This often means allowing individuals to see something for themselves rather than telling or instructing them. There are many types of Coaching/Supporting actions. These can often be described by what the coach is providing to enable greater performance, such as:

Context – conversations that give others the bigger picture. These conversations help to place the person's activity in the context of the activities of the wider department, organization, industry, or country as a whole. In context conversations, the leader is able to share leadership ideas and to make links to how an individual's role and actions fit into that bigger picture. This context sharing broadens an individual's appreciation for their role as well as for the big picture and improves their decision making.

Clarity – conversations that provide clarity do so by providing focus and removing uncertainty without telling an individual exactly what to do. Clarity conversations might be structured around understanding possible outcomes associated with taking or not taking action, or by engaging in active listening to provide feedback without judgment. This conversation may point out choices and possible consequences for various options.

Clarity is personal and is seldom transferred through a telling process – ask questions in order to assure understanding, and remember: it is their clarity being sought in this process, not your clarity.

Demonstration – an example whereby the leader models actions to be learned by the employee. "Walk-the-Talk" is one form of this Coaching/Support role, as is "Showing-by-Doing." Much of what we learn is achieved through an absorption process – we see how others are acting and absorb an understanding without active learning. If the actions we observe are congruent with the spoken leadership values, we "feel" the connection. If the actions are not congruent, we are left with an uneasy, uncomfortable "feeling." Our body telling us that something in what we have witnessed is inconsistent with what we already know. When introducing this new leadership model, or teaching the distinctions of a Perform-and-Learn culture, demonstration of this behavior by a leader is critical to enabling responsibility.

Challenge – acting upon what is blocking an individual's ability to take action. Beliefs and assumptions sometimes create *artificial* constraints that can unconsciously limit performance. A challenge to a team member can be a tough but compassionate intervention in service of the individual's performance commitment. The foundation for a challenge conversation is the employee's performance commitment and the current problem, not an assessment (judgment) and attempt to fix what is wrong with the individual!

Challenge and Support are not mutually exclusive activities. Challenge is a valuable form of support when it is in the service of the individual's performance commitment. Sometimes, it is necessary to be a bit confrontational to help the other person "see" things differently. When a challenge is appropriate, we often use a single question set: "What is the problem?" and "Why is that a problem?" These questions will get repeated until underlying assumptions and personal "truths" that control or limit possibilities for the person are revealed.

Counsel – arises during or after an action that did not meet expectations or when the individual/team is displaying a sense of being overwhelmed, helping staff to regain perspective and providing support while avoiding a transfer of responsibility and/or workload to the leader.

Providing counsel is the process of rebuilding possibilities for the individual or the team, and reconnecting their passions to these possibilities. It is easy to say that a failed possibility gives rise to a new possibility. It is harder for an individual to move from a possibility that did not materialize to a new one without good counsel from their coach.

Counsel is not being a rescuer, however! If you assume this role, you will find yourself overwhelmed and will deny your employees an opportunity for personal growth. Listen with empathy, perhaps allow for grieving and some anger, before beginning the possibility-reconstruction process.

Collaboration – the act of working with the individual as a partner. This may involve exploration or inquiry to jointly solve a problem in situations where the solution must be discovered. Collaborating may also involve the development of a working relationship in which the leader helps the individual practice a new skill.

Collaboration is dependent upon the skills and knowledge of the individuals involved. As a partnering process, it will involve the establishment of joint accountability for outcomes, which is a more personal performance connection for the leader than other coaching activities.

Celebration – perhaps the most fun form of Coaching/Support as it can involve some very creative ways of acknowledging and complimenting contribution as a part of linking actions to Direction. Acknowledgement is important to just about everyone; make it authentic and make it fun, but make it happen!

The Performance Conversation

This leadership model becomes operational through a continuous conversation that focuses on the performance demands of the work. Through this conversation, it is a leader's job to guide individuals into engagement with their work – specifically engagement with the goals of their work. The performance conversation uses all of the elements described above, but it is always connected to the *Direction* element of this leadership model. It is always a future-based conversation.

Engagement is seldom about simply telling. It is not about trading opinions, a situation in which the person with the most authority wins the opinion contest. Engagement involves helping the individual find some element of what they care about, their passion or purpose, within the vision of the enterprise and its goals. It is about helping them identify possibilities that they might create as a result of their contribution to the enterprise's desired future. You can use the Merlin process described in *Chapter 3* to help them create these possibilities. Have them describe how they are delivering performance commitment in the future. Get them to build their own picture of themselves in the future, linking their contribution and passions to the performance goals.

You have talked about hunting rabbits. Now, if you could master these things, what do you think might be possible?

Often, after living with this Merlin-created future possibility, they will be willing to announce their engagement with this future in the form of a performance commitment – a declaration of outcome delivery. One sign of successful engagement will be that the individual feels more capable and sets stretch performance commitments. With this declaration of a performance commitment, the individual demonstrates that he/she is motivated to learn the skills, attitudes, and knowledge necessary to achieve this new goal. The role of the leader then becomes one of keeping this vision alive in the mind of the individual through the use of clarity coaching.

You may be asking, "Is this like a performance appraisal discussion that entails the employee and manager meeting quarterly to set objectives, evaluate progress, plan training requirements, etc.?" The answer is no, not really, as a performance conversation is more comprehensive and less formal. Certainly it should be possible to extract a performance appraisal document from a performance conversation, however.

The performance conversation includes the intent of the performance appraisal discussion, but at a deeper level. In a performance conversation, you are always seeking to find what is missing for the individual if he/she is to maintain engagement with their performance commitment. Here are some descriptive comparators of the two discussions to clarify the differences:

Performance Appraisal	Performance Conversation
Evaluative	Inquisitive
Time limited	Continues over time
Scheduled meetings	Part of every interface
Prescriptive format	Situation specific
System-based	Relationship-based
Hierarchical	Supportive

The key distinction is that the performance conversation will nearly always be forward looking as it is always about tomorrow, what can be done to change or secure the future. The conversation might involve a backward glance, but only when there is a need to pick up some learning that is necessary to alter thinking about the immediate situation.

A performance conversation is a way of being in relationship with the employee, specifically in a relationship centered on performance. This conversation is both supportive and inquisitive, and generally it is a non-judgmental discussion. As this new model unfolds, individuals/teams will move from dependent to independent to interdependent relational stages. Each stage requires differing amounts of Space and different Coaching/Support roles.

To effectively conduct a performance conversation, a leader must have a genuine commitment to the individual's success. In other words, leaders must be authentic about their belief in the ability of each person to learn and to deliver on his or her performance commitment. Belief is not simply about creating stretch goals as part of the Direction. Without buy-in and alignment with the individuals' personal future or their sense of purpose, the participants will see a demand for stretch goals as just another attempt to get more out of them.

When the linkage of goals to personal purpose is missing, the performance conversation will feel like a tug of war between the parties. Comments such as, "Why are you making me do this?" or "I cannot do that unless you train me or give me more authority" will be commonplace. If this occurs, the foundation for the performance commitment is poorly established and a return to the conversation linking the participant's sense of self to the enterprise's vision and goals is appropriate. Perhaps we need to be reminded of the statement attributed to Samuel Butler over 300 years ago: "He who agrees against his will is of the same opinion still." Telling a person what they need to do is not the same as engaging the person in a performance commitment.

Note

1. *This model was originally developed by a group of managers who were struggling to describe a way of working that included new and powerful ways of interacting with people and yet did not lose the common sense practices from the past. Pat Heneghan of ForthRoad Consultancy shared this work with us when we introduced performance management into Abu Dhabi.*

Actions for Enabling Responsibility

The process for keeping everyone (ourselves included) responsible requires that we stay constantly attentive to how choices get made. Following is an activity that will increase your awareness of how you make choices:

1. Keep all of your to-do lists for a one week period of time. Divide the list into activities you assumed were yours to do, activities that might have been done by others and you offered to do, and activities you were asked to do by someone else. First, notice if one list dominates the others – think about what that might tell you about your relationship to responsibility.

2. Look at each list of activities. Was one list more easily completed than either of the other lists? Was your commitment to the tasks on each list the same? What made the difference?

3. Notice future additions to your to-do list. Observe the amount of choice available to you for each new item. When asked to do something, can you make a counter-offer (i.e., "I can do X, but you will have to find someone else to do Y" or "I can certainly do this for you, and if you do this part?")? How helpful would it be to clarify the assumptions you make when accepting or assigning activities?

Seeing activities as choices empowers a person and allows for responsibility. Use this process to help those who work for you as well as to help yourself.

Chapter 5

Every man takes the limits of his field of vision for the limits of the world.
Arthur Schopenhauer

Be in Learning

To *Be in Learning* is more than a transactional process of gathering ideas, tips or techniques from others, but rather, a relational approach to problems. It is about being willing *not* to "know" the answer and an ever present awareness of how our "truths" define problems and limit possibilities. The purpose of this chapter is to explain how to *Be in Learning*.

Think of learning from three different approaches.

- The first approach might be called the **transactional** mode – transferring expertise through training, instruction, or observation. Parental tutoring falls under this model, as do "best practice" applications, and looking for tips and techniques. If you will, transactional learning is to *Be in Class*.

- A second approach might be called the **experiential** mode – applying the transactional instructions, trial and error, analyzing past mistakes for lessons learned, etc. Experiential learning applications often follow transactional learning to create skills and embed knowledge. Experiential learning often establishes our basic rules (beliefs and assumptions) for relating to situations. If transactional is being in class, then experiential is to *Be in Life*.

- Approach three might be called the **inquiry** mode – probing into the unknown to expose assumptions, uncovering new "truths" about old experiences, and developing new distinctions. Inquiry approaches learning from a relational perspective. That is, a problem is defined by our relationship (our beliefs and assumptions) to a situation – a problem gets defined as something that should not be. Inquiry is looking to refine old, or create new, rules of engagement regarding problems. It is in this mode that we actively try to abstract our assumptions and beliefs in order to break the paradigms we are stuck in and to create new insights.

To *be in knowing* (as the opposite of to *be in learning*) is a reliance on transactional and experiential learning. *Being in learning* adds the inquiry mode to our toolset, often as the problem definition step for solution development. It is only when we rise to the level of inquiry that we can truly *Be in Learning*.

A Knowing Leader

A version of experiential learning that compounds the *knowing* position stems from the conventional rule that states, "Leaders are expected to know the answer, or at least to know the source of the answer." Thus, knowing leaders get trapped in a restricted learning loop that drives them to look for known answers to their problems, which effectively condemns them and their organizations to being industry followers and never the leaders.

As an easy test of the degree to which you hold the belief that leaders are expected to know the answer, time how long you are able to remain quiet when you ask a question that is greeted by silence. In other words, when the room stays quiet after a question, how long can you endure the silence before you speak?

Now, think about how you react when you are involved in a meeting in which a leader defines the problem, identifies the causes, and announces the solution? If you consider yourself to be a contributor by nature, you may feel less than empowered and committed in this situation.

There *are* times when knowing the answer is the better approach.

- When another's experience is so limited that they do not know where to start, give them enough direction to start the process.

- When an emergency crisis arises and time is critical, command-and-control the situation.

Then stop. Give yourself permission to *not* have the answer or to be seen as having the answer. Some of the best leaders we have worked with were handicapped by limited experience with the technical aspects of their business. They had lots of business experience, but they were not technically competent in that particular business. This handicap meant that they did not have ready-solutions in hand. Instead, they were forced to be in a learning mindset, listening without judging, and open to inquiry at every turn. In short, they had to see their staff as learning possibilities and interact from this perspective. They were also very aware of their identity and knew what they brought to the table, as discussed in *Chapter 1.*

Knowing is Not Enough

Have you ever worked with someone who would not accept any fact, especially a solution or strategy for a given situation, unless they had experienced it? If they have not done "it" then "it" is not possible – this response drives us up a wall. Their idea of exploring a possibility goes something like, "Well, if you can show me where someone else in our exact circumstances tried 'it,' I will talk with them. But, only if I am convinced will we try 'it'." Forget this strategy ever getting implemented. This person has already defined "it" as a possibility for failure, and if "it" does manage to reach implementation, you can be sure the result will be failure.

Experience is a great teacher, but if experience is an organization's only source of leadership, you can be assured that the organization's future will look exactly like its past. When all decisions are based upon past experiences, the future has already occurred. Just as such an individual might move to a new town and take a new job – it will not matter. Wherever that person goes, his or her past experiences will be there also. Within a very short time, the past will re-emerge. The same holds for an organization whose leaders have this same perspective – relying on the past will yield a future that looks very much like it.

Learning from mistakes is often cited as the surest method for embedding learning, which may indeed be the case but only if we stay aware of the limits of this kind of learning. First, learning is largely available only to the person who made the mistake. Second, unless the context of the mistake is well understood, learning from mistakes can limit future possibilities. "I heard that so-and-so tried that strategy and it did not work."

Introspection on an individual basis is useful and important, and occasionally, a leader might remind an individual to spend a few moments reflecting. Even a team might take a few moments and reflect on what it has learned. However, review is a hindsight action and goals are in the future. Do not spend too long looking backward or you may stumble over the next obstacle on the path forward.

Good news: it's all clear behind us!

Ok, now that we have disparaged the singular use of experiential learning, we can add learning from others to your repertoire. Searching for "Best Practices" as an add-on to personal experience might change the equation and move things forward, but the problems are obvious. Excerpting Best Practices often leads to a piecemeal approach that does not actually integrate a given practice with other business systems. Even if you are successful in transferring knowledge and skills from a source of expertise, it is a catch-up game at best. No matter how fast you are capable of transferring the learning, transactional learning, as the paradigm-of-transfer, defines you as a follower and not a leader.

We are not saying that you should not utilize transactional learning, and we are certainly not saying that you should eliminate experience as a teacher. But a leader needs to recognize that both have their limits, especially given the rate of change in business performance demands we see today. If a repeat of the past is adequate, rely on transactional and experiential learning. If new levels of performance are required, knowing is *not* enough. *Be in Learning* and inquiry learning are necessary adjuncts.

Our Leaps to Truths

Inquiry learning directly challenges the Leaps to Truths that often define our view of reality. To *Be in Learning* means you are open to continually discovering the perceptions that create this current reality, the assumptions that underlie our views: including those assumptions arrived at as reactions to experiences. Discovering the assumptions that are causing certain "truths" involves understanding that reality is created and can therefore be changed.

Over 20 years ago, Chris Argyris,[1] Harvard University Professor of Organizational Behavior, introduced a concept he called our "Ladder of Inference." He used climbing a ladder as a metaphor to describe the leaps we make as regards knowledge: from a simple observation to conclusion of fact, and then the actions we take based on these "facts." He further observed that we climb this ladder without even recognizing our steps along the way.

This metaphor represents a powerful observation of human nature and a tendency that is more likely to affect someone who has a history of successful experiences, as most leaders do. Thus, it is especially important for those in leadership positions to consciously practice to *Be in Learning* to guard against this habit.

We also have a tendency to allow our past experiences to filter our observation of new situations. In effect, we look for evidence to support our experiences – and to ignore other bits of conflicting data that are also present. This action accelerates the rate at which we leap up the steps of the ladder and lock into actions based on history rather than current circumstances. When you believe the wrong things, you do the wrong things – *Possibilities Align Actions.*

Inquiry sets up Possibilities

The inquiry learning mode is designed to interrupt these quick leaps by challenging such truths as the basis for all new problem definitions. The difficulty is that the truths we hold are so strong they are sometimes often difficult to see. The key to unlocking assumptions is a commitment to learning rather than a commitment to being seen as knowing the answer. As this commitment becomes your foundation, you will more readily let go of experience-based truths as absolutes and let them become possibilities.

In fact, inquiry is precisely the process of looking into beliefs that are unknown to us. It is a dialogue without judgment that explores the assumptions defining our current reality. You need to remember that what we know is a very small piece of the universe of knowledge. In fact, much of what we often state as fact are assumptions based upon our experiences. You might think of inquiry as standing on the tip of an iceberg and probing into that vast unknown part of reality that is not easily observable. By exploring or inquiring into this unknown area, we can expand upon the options available to us and thereby find new ways to deal with problems, be they old or new problems.

One way to conduct this inquiry is to use a fact/assumption T-Account situational analysis. Draw a line down the center of a piece of paper and a line across the top. List the facts of some situation on one side of this center line, and on the opposite side list the assumptions you have about the situation. Generally, you will find about five assumptions for every fact. Then take each assumption and "flip it." What if the exact opposite where true? What would the world then look like? How would this different possibility change your approach to dealing with life?

SITUATIONAL ANALYSIS

FACTS	ASSUMPTIONS
• I am five years old	• Bigger is better • The world is flat • Seeing is believing • Dark hides monsters • Parents provide protection • I am the fastest runner ever

Learning about our hidden assumptions is not the same categorically as learning from mistakes or adopting Best Practices from others. In fact, learning about hidden assumptions is a prerequisite to making positive use of any learning from our past or copying others' best practice learning. Discovering one's relationship to a situation is the key to problem identification. Only after the real problem has been defined can experience-based solutions be useful.

By working on problem identification first, and then applying transactional or experiential-based solutions, we position ourselves to make choices and not just react. Choices can be guided by future goals, whereas reaction is based upon past experiences. In fact, we have a choice from the beginning of our dealings with any situation: We have a choice as to how we relate to the problem and the potential solutions. It is this ability to see one's relationship to a situation as a choice that makes it an opportunity for learning. Once the root problem is clear, the type of learning that is required becomes self-evident. Training or applying best practice solutions can then be done within a context that gives these strategies focus and fit as part of a systemic approach.

This learning perspective transforms the enterprise from one that tries to control situations to one that can deal with whatever situation arises. *Being in learning* does not mean setting up situations that we know we can handle, however. In a world of constant change, this is nearly an impossible task anyway. Leaders that are *in learning* balance their situational control efforts with their ability to create new realities when faced with change.

Learning through Stretch

Operation of an enterprise under the guidance of a Living Vision often allows one to make dramatic declarations of Strategic Intent using stretch goals for parts or all of the enterprise's operations. When it is no longer necessary to be in control, to know all the answers up front, leaders create the possibility for propelling learning through this stretch performance process – operating outside of one's comfort zone. Although stretch performance often involves the use of stretch goals, the stretch performance concept is really a disruption of reality, shaking up one's views of the world – a disruption that demands inquiry learning to find solutions that fit this new world.

> *Let us break from the flow of this discussion for a minute to provide a distinction about stretch goals and the disruption of reality. Most of us hold some fixed view of how things "should" work. This is reality for us. As long as we hold these "shoulds" we cannot think of new ways to approach a problem. In order to think differently, it is necessary to disrupt this view. The challenge of impossible stretch goals holds the potential to shake us up so much that we must see the world differently. The goal is so far outside of what we believe is possible that it requires an entirely new belief system – a view of the world that is not possible for us in our normal environment (i.e., relative to our normal goals).*

> *Thus, a true stretch goal cannot have a 50% probability of achievement, or even only a 20% probability, based upon historical norms. A true stretch goal is not possible within our present belief system – the possibility to attain it does not exist. Now, we have a problem that requires us to inquire beyond our current knowledge base. We must disrupt our view of reality in order to solve this problem.*

Stretch performance requires you to use the accountability process to challenge the achievement level of the organization. Stated more specifically, this is a challenge to the organization to set the standards for others in their sector to follow, to break the current rules-of-the-game within their industry. This accountability process sets overarching enterprise-wide stretch goals, and then allows individuals and teams to define their own measurement criteria to achieve these overarching goals. Within the context of the larger goal, this strategy gives the participant some space to develop his or her own specially defined metric(s). This allows individuals to merge their purpose with the performance vision of the enterprise, to maintain the performance connection.

Creating stretch goals for the enterprise and aligning individuals with these goals provides the opportunity for engagement and the declaration of a personal performance commitment – a commitment to be someone they have not been in order to deliver this extraordinary performance. Then, individuals will desire the experimentation and learning required to deliver the results.

A word of caution is in order when using stretch goals to disrupt someone's reality. Until engagement with the possibility has been developed, fear of failure may be the emotion that is evoked. The stretch goal may then elicit a desperate search for reasons why the person or team cannot achieve responsibility for meeting the target. Work toward the target may be approached with built-in excuses right along with a commitment to work hard, as is evident in responses like, "I will try" or "If I work hard, you cannot blame me if the target is impossible – I did my best."

In effect, they substitute a commitment to work hard for a commitment to performance delivery, perhaps approaching the target with incremental improvements to existing systems or copying how others are doing the work (i.e., implementing best practices). After all, they will rationalize, how can you fault someone for failing if they are doing what everyone else in the industry is doing? Now they have two shields to deflect responsibility for missing the target: "We worked hard" and "Everyone else is doing it this way."

In the beginning, the participants may not see the stretch target as an achievable possibility, and until the participants see the target as possible, their actions will reflect trying rather than doing. Until the participants buy-in to the possibility of the target, their energy for the work may ebb and flow with their perception of the chance of obtaining the target. As their coach, a leader may find himself or herself supplying this energy until the target becomes a commitment, and then the energy will become self-generated by the excitement of the goal.

Note

1. *These leaps from observation to truths are based upon the "ladder of inference" concept. Peter Senge, author of The Fifth Discipline, uses the term "leaps of abstraction" to make much the same point.*

Actions for Learning

To *Be in Learning* is a powerful state of being for a leader. It invites others to learn with us and to share their knowledge. In the next chapter, we will show you how to use questions to aid learning, but before you take that next step, we suggest that you try the following activities:

1. Consider the biggest problem you are currently facing. Write down your definition of the problem. Ask yourself, "Why is *that* a problem?" Write down the answer. Ask yourself again, "Why is that a problem?" This time in terms of the previous answer. Write down that answer. Ask yourself one last time, "Why is that a problem?" Again, relative to the previous answer. See if you do not now have a better understanding of the issues that are causing the problem.

2. Take this same problem and make a list of facts versus assumptions, a situational analysis as defined in this chapter. For each of your assumptions, think about what you must believe to be true in order for that assumption to be a fact. Now, assume that the exact opposite is in fact the truth. What would you then assume? This should lead to a very different view of the problem.

Chapter 6

No man ever listened himself out of a job.
Calvin Coolidge

Involve Others in the Conversation

What happens when you listen to someone speak on a topic for more than a minute or two? Even when the topic interests you, do you find yourself agreeing or disagreeing with the person speaking? How much of what is said could you repeat back if asked? For some of us, not a lot of what was said could be repeated, although we seem to be ready to reply with some thoughts of our own. Interesting! Someone is trying to convey their thoughts, but we are busy preparing thoughts of our own.

How often do we find ourselves in the situation of the speaker in this scenario? We desperately want to communicate some important piece of thinking – our vision or an important concept or a message about a client – and tell the other party exactly what we want to say. Later we learn they heard an entirely different message. At that point, we are reminded that it is what is heard that matters, not what is said. What is heard is difficult to manage unless you approach communications from a relational perspective.

Involving others in the conversation puts the relational model into practice during your conversations, and the parties involved *must* make a relational connection for communications to be effective. Involving others in the conversation moves the parties beyond their individual worlds, enabling them to move into each other's context and to acknowledge each other's unique purpose and identity. The relational approach allows for accountability for what is heard, not just what is said.

Think of communication as a message transfer process that occurs through the transmission and reception of words, visual representations, and various unspoken signals. Without a relational connection, these words and signals move from the speaker's world/context into the receiver's world/context without any responsibility on the reception end of the transfer. The purpose of this chapter is to explain how involving others in the conversation stimulates a *perform-and-learn* culture by including context and responsibility in leadership conversations.

To *Involve Others in the Conversation* is deceptively simple. The practice starts with an authentic desire to understand the other person, includes respect for their contribution, and maintains accountability as a continuing component of any relational connection. This relational strategy is put into practice by using genuine questions as the involvement mechanism.

Enabling Listening

In order to involve others in the conversation, you must first "enable listening" – help the other person listen by asking for their contribution. Nothing kills listening quite like being talked at. Nothing enables listening better than a genuine invitation to participate via asking questions – questions that cause the other party to listen.

Enabling listening is more than capturing another person's interest. If you are reading this book, we have your interest, but you might not be listening – listening as in a desire to understand our thoughts. As we write this book, we are constantly reminded that *telling* is the most difficult process for transferring understanding and clarity of thought. Telling seldom causes thoughtful listening.

What occurs for you as we tell you how to make *The Performance Connection?* How are you listening to the words you read? Are you listening more to judge or listening more to learn something? Are you listening for confirmation of your own thoughts on the matter of leadership? Are you looking for flaws and mistakes in our logic?

Obviously, when we tell you something, you are free to choose *how* you listen to what is said or written. We have no ability to guide the choice you make, but if we ask you a question, we can begin to affect how you listen. If we ask you a great question, we might even get our thoughts to pop into your head. We might be able to accomplish thought transfer – the intent of our communications effort.

What happens when we ask you a question? Do you begin to think of an answer? If we could hear your answer, how might this answer cause us to alter our next sentence? How might your answer allow us to be more helpful? If reading this book were an interactive process, we could get to your issues and be more helpful much more quickly. Of course, that would be a two-way exchange, a dialogue, and we could truly involve you in the conversation.

Questions hold the possibility of moving people out of a judging mode and into an active role as a participant in the communications process. By asking a question, the other party is required to take responsibility for listening to your words and the concepts you are trying to convey. You can involve them in a way that requires more than deciding whether you are right or wrong. A genuine question moves the listener out of a purely judgmental mode and into a position of responsibility within the communications arena.

In fact, when we ask others questions as we communicate with them, we open up the possibility for responsibility on both sides of the communications process – we also stand in a position of responsibility for learning from their response. Using questions compels you to listen in return, making the process dynamic. Both parties stand in a position of responsibility for the process and contextual understanding becomes possible.

Learning Context

When we speak, the listener filters our words through their perception of the world – their world of possibilities, their world of language, and their world of experience. What they hear has meaning for them within the context of their identity, their unique being: how they understand words, what their mental models are, what assumptions and beliefs they hold. It is only by listening to their responses and enquiring about their understanding in the interest of greater clarity that we can understand their context – where they are coming from. Until we engage them in conversation through the use of genuine questions, we don't know what understanding they have achieved from the words we used – we do not know the context into which we are speaking.

I'm starving! When is our food coming?

Understanding context allows each party to grasp the other's objectives and to discover shared assumptions, beliefs, and mental models as well as the constraints and influences to which the other person is subjected. This understanding opens up a truly connected relationship. Think of interactions you have with various people. In cases where you have very similar backgrounds and thus can relate well to one another's experiences, do the conversation and connections flow more easily? In cases where the background relationship is less well grounded (e.g., men speaking with women or vice versa), is it more difficult to make this relational connection?

Context and how it defines a common language were never more important than when we introduced performance management to the United Arab Emirates. Although English may be the language of business, English is a second language in the UAE. More importantly, culturally the leadership context is tribal and is overlaid with British bureaucracy due to workplace experience. If you try using business school words to help someone understand how to create an empowering environment, you get a lesson in context – and immediately. As we learned to ask questions, listen, and then speak and act from their context, our interaction became a lot more comfortable.

Dennis was once invited by the General Manager to attend a quarterly board meeting. There was no active participation involved; the topics of discussion were not particularly activities on which he had worked with this organization. He was simply notified by the GM's secretary that he was invited to attend as a guest. Dennis thanked her and said he would try to make the meeting. In his context, this was a business invitation with options, and he responded accordingly: if he was available he would enjoy attending.

When the appointed time for the meeting arrived, he was involved in a meeting with another key client – he was unable to attend. Later that afternoon, he was approached by a member of the General Manager's staff (a friend), who advised that he owed the GM an apology. "Umm, for what he thought?" Ah, the missed invitation. He asked for an appointment to see the GM, and with a slightly longer delay than usually accompanied his requests, it was granted. When he entered the GM's office, he was asked to sit on a sofa, opposite the GM, which was not their usual arrangement – they usually sat next to each other at the GM's round working table. They spoke of the weather – the GM did not ask Dennis how he was! Even as culturally insensitive as Dennis was at the time, he knew that his "relationship" with the GM was broken and he had better start mending it, and fast!

The invitation to the board meeting was the GM's personal way of honoring Dennis for his support over the past year. In the GM's context, missing the meeting was a personal, relational, action that indicated a broken relationship. In Dennis' context, missing the meeting was a loss to himself, but not a loss for the GM – Dennis had other business to do. Context, context, and context. Long story short, Dennis explained how he was engaged in a meeting. The GM said he did not need to apologize – then Dennis really knew what this was about. The GM was telling him that a business excuse is not a reason for failing to honor a personal request. Dennis acknowledged his failure to grasp this context – the personal invitation of "the tribal leader." The GM smiled, graciously explained there was no need to say more, and they moved to his working table.

That was a wonderful lesson in context and communication from a person who lives relational leadership. Once Dennis grasped the GM's context, the lesson was ended and they were back in relationship – business as usual. You hear me, I hear you!

Because our context consumes us by virtue of living in it every day, we need constant reminders to listen first for context when we engage in any communications activity. It is amazing what we learn when we listen to appreciate the other party's context, appreciate it without designating it as wrong or right, just respecting its presence. Unless the other party is involved in the conversation through questions, it is impossible to gain this appreciation for their context.

Helping Responsibility

The art of involving others in the conversation is an effective way of maintaining focus on individual responsibility. By inviting the other person into a conversation, you avoid that natural tendency for listeners to activate their judgment filter as we speak. Involving the listeners in our message via asking them questions avoids the parent/teenager conversation model – the parent speaks in a tone of correction and the teenager listens only for proof the parent is wrong.

Let us take the example of dealing with someone who is often late for meetings with co-workers. How would you approach the supervisory conversation? If you follow the traditional management practice, you might approach them in private and point out the specific action that requires improvement: "I notice that you are often late for meetings." You then might indicate a genuine interest in helping them improve: "Is there some problem you are having that I should know about?" And, you might direct them to improve: "Please be on time for future meetings." And to be certain, this strategy based upon traditional management practices should result in improvement.

However, the relational practice of involving this person in the conversation takes the approach of considering their tardiness to meetings as a relational issue. Contribution Defines Relationships, and what is lost is not only time but this person's contribution. The issue is the performance consequences for the entire group that results from this individual's missing contribution. This individual needs to be invited into the conversation to discuss their contribution relative to accountability for the performance of the others when this person's contribution is missing.

You might start the conversation with a couple of related question: "What are the consequences for meeting outcomes when you are late for a meeting?" and "What are the consequences for the others present at the meeting?" These questions invite the individual to consider their relational accountability to both performance and others. Another question might be, "What happens to your contribution when you are not present?" This question acknowledges their unique value in relationship to the meetings or the team in general. And you might ask, "If you were on time, what might be possible as regards group achievement that is not possible when you arrive late?" This question invites this person to perceive a new possibility in their relationship to the whole.

We do not know how the full conversation may play out, but what we can be sure of is that the employee will be actively involved in a conversation about their relationship to the performance of future meetings. The discussion will not be sidetracked by a story about why they are late, about why being late is really not a problem, or the ultimately annoying excuse: "These meetings never start on time anyway!" The discussion as outlined moves them out of their personal situational context and requires them to take responsibility for the consequences of their actions within a meeting-performance context.

The entire relational conversation keeps the individual responsible for their behavior as it impacts performance, not by you telling this person about it but by this person telling you about it. This conversation limits the opportunity for them to challenge your logic or take you down the history trail with "why" questions.

The traditional management process perpetuates a parent/child relationship. The parent takes responsibility for the child's behavior by pointing it out and demanding corrective action. Possible responses include arguments and defensive statements that challenge the leader's observations about timeliness or justification for the tardiness, including stories about others being late also. It is likely that resentment will be the tone of the discussion, just as when parents confront their tardy teen.

Working out responsibility for themselves!

An involve-others-in-the-conversation approach requires the individual to examine the broader issue of responsibility as well as to consider their relational role with other meeting participants. This requires the individual to remain in a position of accountability for their behavior and yields both performance delivery (bringing their contribution on time) and learning (the meaning of being responsible) as regards future issues.

Helping Learning

Involving people in the conversation by way of questions will cause learning to occur – for both the speaker and the listeners. If you can invite them to build upon the thoughts of those present as well as your ideas, and to not just agree or disagree with a given assertion, it is possible to create something that did not exist for anyone in the room before the conversation started.

Let us say, for example, you want your management team to take on mentoring as part of their management tasks. You might list what a mentor does, how a mentor relates to their mentees, and the outcomes a mentor should achieve. You might even tell a story or two about a mentoring relationship. Your managers will leave with materials describing a mentor, but do they really understand what a mentor does? The most we can know for certain is that they can tell us how *you* described a mentor.

If you are willing to *involve others in the conversation,* you might ask them to develop two lists – one describing a supervisory relationship and the second contrasting it with a mentoring relationship. You might ask them to list what mentoring is and what it is not. Within a two-hour period, the managers will have described in their own language what a mentor does. They will leave with materials describing a mentor, but materials *they* have generated and therefore a description they understand. Moreover, you will also know what each participant understands regarding what a mentor does, and you will know that this is a shared understanding in a common language. They will all implement a common definition and common process when mentoring.

When we use this approach of asking others to define a subject, we are often amazed at what others create, even on topics about which we think we are learned scholars. Once we stop listening only in order to judge and show our superior knowledge, and instead listen to learn, understanding is expanded beyond what just one person knows. Each statement gets built upon by the next person and the learning grows. The language is theirs and not ours, and they do not just offer opinions, but ideas that stimulate other ideas. If we can avoid trading opinions or being in agreement for the sake of looking good, all participants become available to define and solve the problem.

Causing Resistance

Although questions do help involve others, they can also cause resentment and resistance. Questions from a place of judgment, statements in the form of questions, or questions that cause the other party to guess the right answer can be heard as being insincere and inauthentic – perhaps because they *are* insincere and inauthentic.

We speak with more than our words. The context of the conversation, the tone of voice, as well as body language can say more than the words we speak. If there is tension in the air, or if everyone is laughing, these factors can cause the question to be heard quite differently than we intend. Hence, this strategy is more than simply using a question to *involve others in the conversation.* The intent behind the question, in addition to the question itself, provides the opening for involvement.

The "Why did you do it that way?" question may not get you much involvement, if the tone (judging) implies that they did something wrong. If you are open to learning a bit about their thinking, you might say something like, "I am interested in your logic for approaching the problem as you did. Can you tell me your thought processes regarding this fix?" If the inquiry takes place within the context of wishing to learn, even if you are the boss, there is certainly more chance of getting them involved in learning also.

Confrontation versus Discussion

Statements that merely take the form of questions can increase the risk that opinions will simply be traded and the group will ramble around the topic. Let us again consider the topic of mentoring. If you as the boss say, "With the increasing number of young staff and the complexity of our work, don't we need mentoring?" What might be the responses? Certainly, you will not get a "No" answer. You might get something like this, however: "My staff is not a bunch of youngsters" or "I don't think our work is that complex." You are now off the subject of mentoring and into a debate about your logic.

If you have made up your mind, decided that mentoring is the move you want to make, you need to make a statement to that fact. If you have not made up your mind, ask for views without trying to lead the conversation in any one direction: "What would you think about starting a mentoring program? What are some of the pros and cons of introducing such a program?" Have the managers make a list – we love lists for they are a way of getting everyone involved in the conversation. Everyone gets to contribute and everyone has a chance to learn something about mentoring.

If you feel there is only one correct answer to your question, do not ask that question. Tell them what you think is right. Don't make them guess what you have in mind. For example, if a sales person describes a difficult customer to you, and you immediately see how to handle the situation, don't try to make her guess your answer by asking, "What are some of the ways of handling this?" She is probably already frustrated with her attempts to deal with this client and will not appreciate being coached into your already existing solution. Instead, you might say, "I have experienced a situation much like that, and this is what worked for me."

Then ask, "How could you adapt that approach to fit your customer?" This approach:

- Involves her in the solution by respecting her knowledge of the customer,

- Offers a possible solution,

- Leaves you open to learning something about the customer and/or how your sales person thinks.

Leadership is not a classroom in which the test is to find out who knows the correct answer. If the other party feels like they are expected to guess the correct answer, you have missed the goal with your communications efforts. Don't make *perform-and-learn* a game of communication wherein you know the answer and others must learn by guessing what it is. Respect others' contribution and invite them to offer their knowledge so that you might learn also.

Actions for Involving Others

If a picture is worth a thousand words of description, a single question is worth at least five-hundred words of telling. Consider the following actions for involving others in meetings:

1. When you present the agenda at your next meeting, ask the participants what other issues they want to discuss, which gives them an opening to not only convey their agenda but allows them to contribute to yours.

2. Before starting with the first agenda item, ask the participants if there is something they wish to say before the meeting gets started. This allows them to clear their minds of distracting thoughts and will make them more willing to participate.

3. If a topic is new to the group and people have different levels of understanding about the background for the discussion, rather than telling them what you think others know, ask group members to share their background on the topic. This immediately involves everyone in the discussion and allows you to understand the context for your agenda item.

Destination Defines the Path

I f you do not know where you are going, then any road will get you there." This truism comes to mind as we consider the importance of this second element in the Relational Management Model, the definition of which bears repeating here:

- **A Living Vision and Strategy** provides the performance vision and identifies Strategic Intent for organizational focus. These are the organization's ***purpose*** and ***identity*** statements, the foundation upon which organizational performance is built, but these are also the foundation upon which the individual stands as a part of the organization.

The living *vision* and *strategy* are the context for an organization's relational leadership model. The vision and strategy parts, or the statement of the organization's future, are very common in most sustaining enterprises. The *living* part, or the connection that drives personal and leadership decisions, is less common but more important.

Humans desire a sense of the future – to see a meaningful connection to a future possibility. Relational leadership accesses this human need by connecting the individual to this vision – a word picture that declares future aspirations – and brings that sense of the future to life in the present for the organization by anchoring the vision in the reality of today. Hence, we add the term *living*. This living vision serves to guide the collective organization and becomes a future within which each individual can find a connection with their life's passion.

When we speak of a living vision and strategy, we are not talking about some apparition, a dream of paradise, or about some wall-mounted statement developed during an executive getaway. A living vision and strategy is about understanding the core of what your enterprise delivers to its customers (in the present and as envisioned for the future) and the framework for its delivery that clarifies direction while allowing for discovery. In other words, a living vision and strategy is a prediction of the future – an articulation of the future as a possibility stated as concepts that can be practiced today.

This living vision is an engaging description of the enterprise that weaves the elements of core values, markets served, or products delivered into a living picture. It is a declaration of the enterprise in the present and in the future, and in this last regard, it includes measurable goals that serve to describe the enterprise in the future – the basis for the accountability system.

There are three critical reasons for maintaining a living vision and strategy:

1. To anchor the organization in the future rather than the past, which requires unusual clarity of purpose and direction. It creates a pull on the organization that makes business-as-usual unacceptable, and it allows for possibilities beyond an historical perspective.

2. To create a new paradigm through which individuals can see the world, which allows enterprise staff members to see external events in a new light, giving them new meaning and significance. It serves as a filter through which the organization can sort out the choices regarding what it will pursue.

3. To provide a personal connection to the enterprise for individual purpose and passion as a possibility. A resource for people to find answers to the questions: "What is in this for me?" and "How does this work touch my heart?" and "Why do I want to work with this organization?"

This connection to the future is vital. While it is likely that most of us would say we live in the present, facts suggest that we live largely in the past. That is to say, we use historical experiences to interpret the present and to construct our view of the future. A vision that includes both a picture of the enterprise in the future and the present challenges this traditional perspective – pulling individuals and organizations forward.

Chapter 7

Where there is not a vision, the people perish.
Proverbs 29:18

Defining the Destination

Direction is important for any management model, but this is doubly true for the relational model. Within this relational model, each Me Inc., team, group, unit, and etc. connects their business purpose to the *Direction* of the enterprise, and the accountability system must be built on the foundation of this *Direction* element. In this chapter, we are going to provide a conceptual framework for developing and implementing the various elements of enterprise-wide *Direction*. This chapter will also set the stage for presenting the other elements of the relational model, specifically the business-purpose team structure and the accountability system.

Direction is a rather comprehensive term that goes by many other names – Mission, Vision, Strategy, Goals and Objectives – and has many meanings within business literature. We are here emphasizing the "living" aspect of the relational model to point out the importance of maintaining the dynamic connection between the organization's direction and stakeholders in the face of constant change for both individuals and the enterprise. As we connect the conceptual living vision to strategy and business planning, and then to the very tangible operating budget, we are going to expand *Direction* to include the goals element. We are going to use the term *Living Performance Vision* to add goals in order to emphasize the need to keep *Direction* alive as the environment and each individual's perspective change. If you are a student of strategic concepts, this term, *Living Performance Vision*, is much the same as the concept of "Strategic Intent" introduced by Hamel and Prahalad in their groundbreaking May-June 1989 Harvard Business Review[1] article of the same name.

The linkage of our *Living Performance Vision* to an enterprise's daily operations is shown in the following illustration:

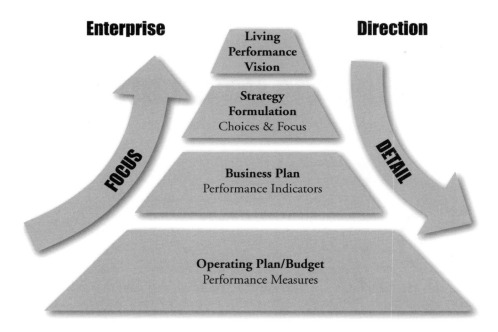

Through its measurable connection to daily business, the *Living Performance Vision's* job is to keep pulling your enterprise forward – from its current state toward its desired (or required) state of being – as your world evolves.

To ensure its relational context, this broad *Direction* element needs to contain each of the three perspectives defined previously – heart, head, and hands. This *Living Performance Vision* should beckon the heart with a purpose-driven future. It should give distinction to the enterprise, an identity that sets it apart and gives people a clear understanding of who the enterprise is in their marketplace. And this *Direction* element should contain a declaration of performance accountability.

For *Direction* to do all of this, the process must involve each of the elements. There must be what we will call a *Transactional* element of process, whereby the hands collect data – a prescriptive bit of gathering and assembling. There must be an *Intellectual* element of process, whereby the head sorts, assimilates, and learns. And there must be an *Intuitive* element of process, whereby the heart absorbs and lives with the possibilities presented. Of course, all of these processes can be present during the same activity, and in fact, it may be a requirement that all three are at work in each step. In the final stage, however, the head and heart direct the hands to write the well-worded statement that will call the organization into the service of the *Living Performance Vision*.

Development and implementation of a *Living Performance Vision* is not a simple process that lends itself to a step-by-step formula. In fact, a formula of any type is not sufficient. Rather, the *Living Performance Vision* consists of the application of the right process under the right conditions at the right time. We can hear your complaints now: "Oh, that is very helpful – saying the development process depends." Let us explain. Your performance vision is *your* performance vision for *your* enterprise within *your* industry. That is, the development process is, in part, an integration of your identity with the conditions of the enterprise and the industry, and thus, the state of the organization, the state of the industry, and the identity of leadership will all influence the development process.

In other words, it is all about alignment – alignment of those three relational factors with the environment and the person. For any size enterprise, the leadership persona is so important that even the vision and strategy development processes cannot ignore the identity and passion of the leader, which means that, using the Relational Management Model in the real world; leaders get to modify the process to maintain that alignment of factors. Consequently, as you read on, we will ask you to think about how you would respect the three basic relational laws and four leadership practices while adapting the Relational Management Model to your persona and your specific environment.

We are going to start with the vision portion of the process, working through the strategic choices involved and the focus process. The more detailed planning elements will be covered as part of the accountability system.

Vision Lights the Way

Why is what you do important to you, your employees, your suppliers, and your customers? Your *Living Performance Vision* should describe your purpose with such breadth and clarity that each of these stakeholders can find their answer to that question. As the guiding light and foundation for your *performance connection,* you want this articulation to inspire, guide, and define the enterprise as a possibility.

A *Living Performance Vision,* if it is real, is 'heart' stuff. If it is just statements for an office wall placard or a marketing brochure, it is 'head' stuff. Stated from a slightly different perspective, without a meaningful *Living Performance Vision,* the organization has no heart – and thus no place for people to connect their hearts. The words of the *Living Performance Vision* are the first step for guiding people toward connected action – it establishes the intention of the enterprise in its relationships to customers, employees, suppliers, regulators, and etc.

Because this is heart stuff, not only is the process of developing a *Living Performance Vision* critical but so is the process by which stakeholders will grasp its meaning for them. It is a rare case that the bare words are so beautiful, so inspiring, so capable of filling one with awe that people feel their connection to the enterprise just by reading them. The heart connection is personal, an individual connection, and just like any relationship, it must be lived with for a while to see both the positive and the negative in its application and to move it from the head into a heartfelt position.

We'd bet that everyone reading this book has some form of a vision statement. However, since it is the guiding light for the Relational Management Model, it is important that the light works as we are defining it here. It is our experience that at least some portion of vision work should undergo redefinition every few years. No, the mission of the enterprise should not change – unless that mission has been accomplished. Indeed, the core purpose and core values established previously may not change, but the external world and your view of it will change inevitably. The process of redefining the vision will give you a fresh set of filters through which you process external data.

The development process for a *Living Performance Vision* cannot be entirely independent of strategy formulation, although the primary work on the vision should precede the bulk of strategy development. Here is a summary of a *Living Performance Vision* development process for a team:

- Start with some understanding of the world in general and what is changing – listen to a few futurists and read some articles on factors that are driving change. Bring some people with radically different backgrounds to speak to your organization. They may provide very different perspectives on the future of the world, your industry, and your organization. Immerse the entire team in thinking about change, and then ask everyone to contribute to a list of changing factors confronting the enterprise.

- Using these factors, stand 5 or 10 years in the future and tell a story of what is happening in the world – specifically the world around your enterprise. Ask others to build on the initial story, adding twists and turns to expand the possibilities. Now, tell a new story that is exactly the opposite of the first one. For example, if technology integrates cultures in the first, it separates them in the second.

- Now, consider your basic purpose as an enterprise. How is it affected by these new worlds? What are the societal needs created or challenged by this future and how do these impact your enterprise? What might you supply to society under these conditions? Create a variety of purpose statements – mix, match, and blend ideas to get a statement that has some feelings in it. Give a purpose that is felt but without belaboring the point with numerous words. Use simple elements that convey large ideas, like:

  ➤ *A Place Where Healing Begins* – for an addiction treatment agency

  ➤ *To Power the Nation* – for an energy provider

  ➤ *Keeping America Rolling* – for a trucking firm or tire producer

  ➤ *Dressing Women for Success* – for a women's retail clothing store

  There is benefit beyond the obvious in these purpose-driven statements. They look toward the end value for the customers and thereby ground decision-making at all levels.

- Move to the values that fit with you and this future. Values are *the* defining characteristics of your governance frame, or filter. List, define, challenge and debate changes, deletions, and additions to what you have held as values, and then add the values frame to the purpose statement.

> ➤ *A Place Where Healing Begins. Holistically empowering people, through dignity and respect for human frailty.*

> ➤ *To Power the Nation. Delivering environmentally compatible energy to improve life for our people.*

- Then move to some relative performance concepts. How will you measure progress? Will you be recognized as the industry leader? The goals element of a vision, the piece that can be measured, is vital due to its link to accountability.

- Now write some statements regarding your enterprise as a possibility in these futures. How do you serve society? What is the value you add? Connect your purpose to your stakeholders and to your values – define your enterprise through its relationship to the stakeholders, including this last performance element.

> ➤ *A Place Where Healing Begins. Holistically empowering people, through dignity and respect for human frailty. Delivering an industry-leading success rate of clients with chemical-free lives.*

- Then have each member of the team write a personal version of the vision, incorporating how this lives for them personally, how it connects to their passion.

Now, you have either confirmed the existing definition of the enterprise or you have some work to do moving the new one upward (to the Board of Trustees/Directors), outward (to suppliers and customers), and downward (to employees) so this vision can do its work of pulling you forward.

But wait, it is not time to print the new placards yet. Because this is heart stuff, and we are not always sure what our heart is saying (again, you will need to live with this vision for awhile), it is often useful to set aside the *Living Performance Vision* and let the *Strategy Formulation* (head stuff) make it more definitive or meaningful. In other words, after getting the key players on the same page regarding a *Living Performance Vision*, let their specific definitions evolve as *Strategy* unfolds. Start on *Strategy Formulation* while the *Living Performance Vision* is gelling but before it has hardened. The words may gain new meaning or, as strategy work unfolds, change to give better definition and guidance to the organization.

Make it Personal

While you are living with the words and working on Strategy Formulation, broaden the conversation about the *Living Performance Vision* with the organization. Work downward first rather than upward. Board-approved visions are generally fixed in stone. The relational model is not a "tell them" what to believe but a "connect them" through conversation model.

To capture their hearts and thus make this a true living vision for them, your description must be open enough to allow for a cascading effect: the vision gets more and more tangible at each level in the organization while staying connected to the levels above, and each individual is in turn connected to their team's vision, which is described within the context of the business unit's vision.

> *For example, an upscale retail store's Home Department has a vision of providing a "visual living experience" for customers. Sales associates with a zeal for creative design find passionate expression in the opportunity to develop and maintain the floor inventory in visual-display mode. These employees blend arrangement, color, and space to present merchandise in eye-catching glory. However, sales associates, whose purposes are more related to personal connections, find their passionate expression in helping customers experience their home-decorating plans by presenting them with home accessory mix-and-match options.*

You cannot talk groups of people into an aligned purpose. Likewise, simply requiring people to read the vision statement or interpreting for them what the vision means does not accomplish this task either. In fact, actions are not aligned by what *you* say is possible; actions are aligned by what *the employees* believe is possible. The connection between a personal passion and an enterprise's vision must also be personal. The manager of this Home Department must work with each sales associate to help them see and feel the connection to this vision.

You might try running a series of workshops, letting staff play with the concepts. Tell them shortened versions of the future-world stories, or make a film of the leadership workshop so they can also hear the stories you heard – let them add bits and ask them what a changing world might mean for the enterprise. Give them various statement options to consider – ask them how each one might affect them differently. The feedback may even be informative. Some of your employees might be much better equipped to understand a changing future than you imagine. Think about doing this exercise with companies in the 1970s who had an employee with a passion for computers. What possibilities might they have opened up in such a session?

After working with staff, it is time to move upward and bring the Trustees/Directors on board. These people also need a personal as well as a common definition of how the *Living Performance Vision* defines the enterprise. They will not get this common definition by voting on wording statements, however. Take them through a mini-workshop wherein they must articulate the meaning of the words and agree on the framework created by this Living Vision. Then you can print the new placards.

Early staff involvement will make it easier to cascade the final work and for the *Living Performance Vision* to be understood. However, the *Living Performance Vision* will indeed only live for the organization to the degree the words integrate with other organizational processes. Take the example of the department store that has the "visual living experience" for their shoppers as their vision of their enterprise. Although sales associates were encouraged to live their creative passion through how they display stock, when the accountability system failed to recognize time spent on display creation and only measured sales per hour, the connection quickly faded. In short, connecting the head, heart, and hands requires an integration of systems. When systems send conflicting messages, the connection is at least weakened and often broken.

Make it Live

Even if all the systems reinforce the vision, alignment is still not a one-time event. We do not live in a static world. The magnitude of "pull" due to aligned possibilities, the gravitational effects of each on the other, is directly proportional to the clarity of the possibilities – the connection to the vision. Time and the accumulated impact of minor changes begin to cloud our view of possibilities. Every time there is change in the enterprise – such as offices merging, a new division or activity beginning, hiring a new leader – individuals may begin to define differing possibilities. As time progresses and both the internal and external environment change, all employees will need to be individually and collectively reconnected in a meaningful way.

Staying connected – the hard way!

It is often tempting to give employees advice about a changing environment, or even to tell them not to worry about change. However, offering them *your* clarity is of little value, as it is *their* clarity as regards the possibility that change represents that is important – and they must arrive at the words to represent their personal meaning. For much of the organization, change may only mean that differing positive possibilities need to be aligned. For example, the recent success of a program or winning a new contract may mean different possibilities for different individuals – at least as they define them. You may even see the possibilities differently than the staff does. Without realignment, everybody may take off in different directions. In conversations with your staff, ask them the following:

- What has changed for them?
- What is most worrying to them at the moment?
- What must happen to overcome this concern?
- What is the goal they are seeking?
- Who shares this goal with them?
- What new actions can they take?
- What will they need to do differently?

The need to connect an individual's passion to the overall vision for the enterprise is important when hiring as well, or indeed when you transfer an employee to a new assignment. When hiring new personnel, employers often emphasize an experience-based résumé. This is indeed a great way to discover what the person has accomplished and their historical-experience base, but it does not tell the story of their purpose or identity. Instead of just talking about past jobs, explore a potential employee's history from the perspective of their purpose or passions in life relative to your vision. Each time you engage a new employee, or transfer, or promote a person, require them to write a vision statement. Ask the interested parties to tell you what they see as possibilities in this new work. Take time to discover if the individual's statement of themselves and the corporate performance vision can even be aligned *before* they are hired or transferred to a new assignment.

Vision provides direction and connection, but vision can get clouded, and at times we are in need of corrective lenses. Each time there is a change, large or small, it is necessary to re-engage people with the vision so that relationships are built and maintained upon a common view and common goals.

Note

1. *For further understanding of how contribution drives effective vision and strategy development, you may wish to read the May-June 1989, Harvard Business Review article titled, Strategic Intent, by Gary Hamel and C.K. Prahalad. We believe this is the original basis of the "Vision-Driven" craze that has swept the organizational development landscape over the last 15 years. The Strategic Intent concept is entirely compatible with this relational leadership model.*

Chapter 8

Opportunities multiply as they are seized.
Sun Tzu

Learning the Path

S trategy is the bridge between vision and action. It sets the context for the necessary tactical actions to deliver the organization's contribution to its customers' value chain. At its most basic level, *Strategy* is about **"what you sell and to whom you sell"** or **"what you contribute and to whom you contribute."** At the operational level, *Strategy* is a series of differentiating activities (the enterprise's identity, as in what distinguishes you from every other competitor) that support the delivery of the vision. *Strategy* is the story of how the enterprise will leverage this identity.

The value of *Strategy* as "what you contribute and to whom" is simplicity. What is often a complex conversation in the face of continuous confrontation and confusion due to the turbulent external environment is reduced until you achieve absolute clarity. That is, the organization needs to understand its identity, even while that identity continues to grow and evolve, in order to respond to external environmental change – and *Strategy* in this regard allows such an understanding in the simplest possible terms.

However, this is not to suggest that your strategic planning is simple and that it does not take place on multiple planes. This is to say that your identity needs to be clear to both your employees and your stakeholders – even as you continue evolving it. The constant evolution of your *Strategy* gives it layers of complexity, and often this can contribute to more than a bit of confusion about the enterprise's ultimate intention. Strategic thinking on the part of the organization, guided by the leadership team, never stops. Thus, leadership must be constantly scanning the environment, processing the data it finds, and transforming that data into information for use in the organization's *Strategy Formulation* process.

It's a whatdoyoucallit!!
What change does it mean for our organization?

As the new information is absorbed, another layer of strategy may be developed and added. We describe these layers as the declared strategy (active strategy that gives the organization its clarity of purpose, its identity), and the evolving strategy (migration or evolution of strategic thinking as the organization learns from implementation and this environmental scanning). It is the declared strategy that the accountability system uses to provide clarity and to focus downward and across the organization.

Strategy tells the organization how the enterprise's core competencies (again, identity) will be used to build and maintain its competitive positioning.

- Identity, based on price for example, drives a low-cost strategy and operational excellence as a core competency – think Wal-Mart for example.

- Identity based on promotion indicates a strategy of product leadership and a core competency of creative innovation – think Intel for example.

This understanding of what the organization offers its customers then allows those employees with direct customer contact to identify and seize strategic opportunities – maintaining strategic focus while maneuvering the strategy as customers' needs change.

Your strategy-based, scorecard-type accountability system will be designed to guide this identity focus process, but the organization also needs regular reinforcement from leadership. The method for reinforcing contribution is quite simple. Every time you request information or decide on a policy application, ask yourself, "How does this action focus the organization on our strategic contribution equation? How might we apply this policy so it respects contribution as the driver of our customer relations?" Then, when working with staff members, regularly ask them how their work relates to this customer contribution relationship.

Strategy Formulation

Strategy Formulation is not merely planning, but listening, learning, and thinking in the service of planning. Thinking gives the context for planning the enterprise, and planning sets the context for managing the enterprise. Thus, planning links the head (strategy) and the hands (accountability).

Strategy formulation is the process of looking for *new insights* that will allow the enterprise to develop a competitive advantage, and since competitive advantage is generally a fleeting thing (others are busy copying almost as fast as one enterprise invents), the search is non-stop. Strategy formulation is about learning – understanding realities about the business, competitors, customer values, and the external environment – and strategy formulation is about learning faster than your competition. As part of strategy formulation, the enterprise clarifies what it sells (i.e., intellectual property, tangible products, services) and to whom (target markets). And in the process, facts and issues not previously known by either the organization's leaders or competitors will be discovered. In short, strategic formulation is about learning as a leadership team and learning as an organization.

Strategy Formulation might use one of three philosophies in the process of searching for these *new insights* and clarifying what the organization should sell and to whom:

1. **Operations Philosophy** uses tools such as Competitor Analysis, Consumption or Value Chain Mapping, Benchmarking, Total Quality Management, and even Re-engineering processes.

2. **Futuristic Philosophy** uses Technology Mapping, Scenario Analysis, Competitive Strategy Analysis, and even Chaos Theory.

3. **Behavioral & Cultural Philosophy** uses such tools as Enterprise Visioning and Empowerment and Organizational Learning tools to forge *strategy* as the organization navigates within its ever changing environment.

None of these techniques is best, but rather, choosing which to use is situation-specific. The choice of the application depends on the state of the particular business, the current environment for that industry, as well as the identity of the leadership. Strategy formulation is a process of looking for what is missing from your existing knowledge base, which is of course a tough mandate – finding out what you do not know when you do not understand what you do not know. This sounds confusing, but in reality, this is a process of looking for something you cannot define – an unknown object that you will only recognize when you see it or feel its presence. Thus it is important to try different processes. You need to *do* different things in order to *learn* new things.

Once you have recognized this need for learning, a good rule to guide your actions is to use the philosophy with which the organization is *least* comfortable. Move outside of your comfort zone and use individuals with differing backgrounds. Seek individuals with differing contributions to build the teams that will work on the Strategy, seek challenge from outside the enterprise, and look at other industries – dissimilar benchmarking can be very powerful. See what enables others to achieve different results in different circumstances.

However, this is not to suggest that you should imitate others in your industry – the herding instinct is strong. The law of competition setting standards does not make it the law for strategy formulation. Strategy is not about standard performance but about customers and your contribution to their value chain. We all know that it is easy to think you can avoid criticism by doing what everyone else is doing, but you will also fail to provide strategic leadership by following the herd. In your leadership role of scanning, visioning and strategy formulation, you should be figuring out ways to redefine your products and services in order to become the industry trendsetter.

In short, a successful long-term strategy must be more than the pursuit of industry trends. A leader is the trendsetter, not the trend-follower. Leadership teams that analyze data in a search for evidence to support existing practices are not looking to learn or to create insight. These are *knowing* leaders who are looking to prove themselves right. Their thinking comes from the past, not the future. They are looking backwards, looking to justify past decisions. Do not get caught up in being right. Keep challenging the thinking until new thoughts, "aha's", begin to appear – that is the sign to proceed with the next step: choices and focus.

Choices and Focus

After sorting data, mapping the past, present, and/or future by whatever process you follow, some clarity should start to emerge. If not, it is time to *make* some clarity emerge. Remember, clarity is not certainty, however. At the pace of change with which an enterprise must deal today, certainty is probably an illusion anyway, or at least a quickly passing reality. Clarity is sorting out what is important. Informed by the analysis process, it is time to integrate the data about the enterprise, customers' values, competitors, etc. and develop clarity.

- What are the enterprise's core competencies?

- How do these competencies deliver what the customers value?

- What customers are you positioned to better serve than your competition and why?

- What products and/or services will meet these customers' needs?

- What customers should you not be serving and why?

- What products and/or services should you not be offering?

- Where are you undecided and need to continue strategy formulation?

The answers to the previous questions should establish more clarity about the *Direction* of the enterprise as a whole. Deciding what *not* to do is almost as important as deciding what you *are* going to do. This work is about choices and focus and the result is clarity. Revisit the *Living Performance Vision* and make sure the statements are consistent. Perhaps more importantly, make sure that your *Living Performance Vision* is still a useful statement, providing internal guidance and external clarity about who you are as an enterprise.

Strategy formulation is an ongoing process and will not have an end. As some clarity emerges, apply the 80/20 rule and allow the enterprise to move forward, even as uncertainty exists in some areas. It is far better to accept that some questions are unanswered than to falsely believe – and send the signal to the organization – that leadership has all the answers. Having some unanswered questions will ensure that the leadership team continues environmental scanning and the strategic formulation process. You might call this return loop the "strategic conversation," a discussion that continues for the entire life of the enterprise.

This activity of strategy formulation is hard work. It involves subtle, perhaps sophisticated thinking, and even some subconscious processes, but in truth, after strategy formulation has provided you with insights and focus is when the real work begins – getting the organization to live the strategy. The key process for bringing the strategy to life is the Accountability System, which signals the Strategic Intent to the organization via cascaded metrics, milestones, and targets throughout the enterprise.

The development of complete metrics and milestones will be part of Business Planning, a more detailed activity. This should include an actual numbers-driven strategic plan and/or a 5-year forward business plan. The performance indicators developed from the Business Planning work are important to provide assurance that the strategic roadmap is providing good *Direction* and/or to highlight areas where change is necessary. The short-term performance targets for these metrics will be identified as part of the Operating Plan/Budget development.

Before we discuss more about how Strategy is linked through the Accountability System, it may be useful to look at the relational model's structural element – **A Business-Purpose Defined Team Structure.**

Me Inc. as an Organization Chart

H ave you ever felt that your organizational structure impeded performance? How often have you changed the structure only to find that improvement from the change was short-lived or non-existent? Both of these things happen because of the traditional use of organizational structure as a division of labor and as the foundation for position power. The Relational Management Model uses strategy to set the structural framework and then builds the organization on a foundation of the Me Inc. concept. We call this:

- **A Business-Purpose Defined Team Structure,** which establishes an entrepreneurial, market-driven internal environment for the enterprise. Me Inc. is a free-market paradigm that is usually forced to fit into an authoritarian concept. Business-purpose designed team structures help return free-market concepts to the organization and thus enable an alignment with the Me Inc. paradigm.

Structure is a necessary element of every organization. Whether it is called an organizational chart or table of organization; whether it is described by layers of boxes with solid or dotted connecting lines or intertwined egg shapes to reference a team atmosphere; whether it is centralized, de-centralized, functional, product line driven or uses matrixes; whether it is formal or informal, every organization requires a structure that provides a framework for configuring its activities.

As a division of labor, organizational structure should have the advantage of accountability and clarity, but when designed and implemented as a position-based structure it has the disadvantages of isolation, insulation, and inflexibility as it transforms organizations into silos that cut-off relationships. When structure establishes sections, departments, divisions – all words rooted in separation rather than cohesion – it signals those in the organization to divide rather than unite.

Unfortunately, for most of us, our organizational experience, along with traditional "job" descriptions, program us to function within our organizations from a position basis. When people focus primarily on their position, they have little sense of responsibility for the impact of their actions on others. After all, they did not construct the organizational design. If they are disconnected from the larger purpose of the enterprise, they are likely to feel little responsibility for this loss of connection. The result is insulation, organizational inflexibility, and relationships defined primarily by position.

If you only knew what I know about this organization..... ...

As a framework for configuring its activities, structure is both a strength and a weakness. It provides a measure of control and clarity for areas of responsibility, but without relational connectivity, structure can impede the interdependency requirement for organizational success. However, relationships based on contribution introduce a relational aspect and will soften the tendency for divisional separation, but this addition alone will not make divisiveness go away. The purpose of this section is to describe how to create and integrate structure so that it works with relational leadership to deliver interdependency and accountability.

For structure to be an integrating rather than dividing force, the macro-structural frame must flow top down from the strategy, but with this structural frame being filled bottom up using the Me Inc. concept. At this micro-level, each organizational position becomes a unique business with an identifiable contribution. *Business-Purpose Defined Teams* bring these two elements together, establishing an entrepreneurial, market-driven internal environment for the enterprise. Me Inc. as an individual business allows for measurable, market-driven accountability at every level. This unique business identity arrangement allows *Competition Sets the Standards* to work as the basis for performance measurement.

Chapter 9

To find a fault is easy; to do better may be difficult.
Plutarch

Building the Structural Frame

T here is no right structure for any organization. In fact, there should seldom be a fixed structure. Structure should depend on strategy (as in the old organizational axiom: "From strategy flows structure"), and thus, structure should continuously transform as strategic thinking progresses. Structure will also depend on the organizational maturity of the culture, and it should operate with less rigidity as the organization learns that responsibility is about being accountable for the impact your actions have on others. In other words, structure becomes more malleable as an organization learns interdependency. Structure may be considered one of the hard, or fixed, elements of the organization, but under our Relational Management Model, the fixed time period is only as long as business conditions remain fixed.

With a relational leadership model, structure will also depend on the *identities* of the key leaders, and in its detail, structure will probably depend on the history of the organization and its sacred cows. We realize that saying "it depends" is not a particularly useful tool for helping others get into action, so we have criteria for making structure support this relational model:

- First, connect the framework structure for the organization to your strategy. Construct *Business Units* that reflect or relate to key strategic business drivers. A strategic business unit might focus on one class of customers, or one unit might deliver one element in your activity's value chain or produce one group of products or services. Or if your enterprise is small and has only one strategic driver, the entire enterprise might be a single business unit. We will offer you guidelines in a moment to help you distinguish strategic business units.

- Second, within these business units, try thinking of your organization as a collection of *Internal Enterprises*. These internal enterprises might be as small as a single person (think independent contractor concept) or as large as say a 30-50 person group (think entrepreneurial small business concept). Each enterprise must have a product or products/service or services they specialize in, as well as an identifiable customer base.

- Third, require each internal enterprise to write a *Business Purpose* statement for their business and have their customers confirm this as a useful statement of purpose. Include some element of identity – what this internal enterprise brings that is unique to their market – in this purpose statement.

- Fourth, introduce a *Market Process* (which can be internal or have external elements) for managing this relationship between customers and suppliers. Use a process that demands accountability from both parties, the sellers and the buyers, for performance toward the greater good of the organization.

- Fifth, form *Leadership Teams* in which members hold collective accountability for the aggregated performance of internal enterprises and/or business units.

- Sixth, use *Shared and Common Performance Measures* as part of your accountability system and link a bonus element of compensation to these shared and common measures.

- Lastly, change the *Language*. To avoid the language of separation, we use *Unit, Group, Team,* or even *Community* to describe these internal enterprises. However, let's not fool ourselves. Calling employees "Associates" who are members of a "Customer Solutions Group" may have some impact, but this impact will be of little lasting value unless it is part of a broader integrated relational model. Names alone do not change a culture, as cultural norms get their behavioral signals from a larger variety of sources than just their names.

The organization and its business teams are designed to focus on their markets (customers, products, services), whether these markets are external or internal. Without market accountability, the players (by whatever names they are given) will quickly establish internal processes that serve their own needs rather than the needs of their customers or the organization as a whole.

This market design structure is interconnected as follows: each internal enterprise's purpose is linked to its customers' needs, its identity is linked with what the internal enterprise brings to their market, accountability is linked with how they address these needs, and their customers' accountability is linked with how they *respect* these internal enterprises' place within the greater organizational community. This business-purpose team concept produces an entrepreneurial/market-driven way of life throughout the organization – whatever its size.

Miss Markets, may I introduce you
to our Relational Model!

The criteria we have outlined for you and this market design attend to the three relational elements – purpose, identity, and accountability – for each internal enterprise. These elements are critical for the use of free-market relationships between internal enterprises as the foundation for avoiding the forces of structural separation. Note that in organizations where internal enterprise costs are allocated on some average cost basis, these conditions of purpose, identity, and accountability are seldom met.

> *We worked with one organization in which an average cost allocation process was used for internal service department billings. The result was constant internal bickering and repeated demands for cost reduction by one group of customers whose external market pricing could not bear the high cost of services. Interestingly, other internal customers (at a different place on their product lifecycle maturity curve) were satisfied with the costs and the corresponding high quality of service they were getting. The solution was to introduce a market process for determining services and costs. The internal service providing enterprise drew up a menu of service options – one star for basic service to five stars for integrated, value-adding services. A clear scope of work was described for each level of service, along with a corresponding cost. The customers could choose a service level, but they only got the scope of work they paid for – not three-star costs with demands for five-star service. There were some minor adjustments to the process of buying services to avoid large peaks and valleys in the service demand levels, but different business units were able to match their service (and cost) needs to the maturity of their product lifecycle – a good example of using a market process to manage the relationship between internal buyers and internal sellers of services.*

Markets demand accountability and establish framework-type structures that overlay the organizational structure. Placing the internal teams within the same market-driven environment of the larger enterprise allows leadership to define business outcomes as the criteria for *Direction* and control. Market discipline then flows vertically through the organization – from Me Inc. at the foundation level to business units at the strategic or corporate level – providing a unique focus on performance. Individual responsibility is enforceable without micromanagement or subjective judgment.

Look at how your enterprise is structured. What products/services and customers are associated with each section, each department? How do you describe the products/services and customers of the various committees and/or councils involved in managing the enterprise? Now return to your *Living Performance Vision* and your strategy description. How would you describe each group's relationship to this *Living Performance Vision?* What customers does each division, department, group, etc. serve? If there is a lack of clarity or if you cannot readily identify their customers or products, there is a high probability that the structure will not support a relational model with market-driven accountabilities, and of necessity, some restructuring will be a part of your enterprise's transformation into this relational world.

A business that wishes to transform into a relational leadership model must transform its structure toward Business-Purpose Defined Groups, a structure wherein customers, products and services are clearly identified – even for the leadership team(s). Start the structural transformation by looking at every group within your enterprise as a business rather than as an activity center or function. Before you take this step, however, you must look at your strategic drivers to identify organizational Business Units – the next topic.

The Business Unit

If your enterprise is a small business, it is quite possible that this business unit concept is not applicable – the enterprise *is* the business unit. In this case, as an organization, there is a single strategic driver. If so, move on to considering the various business teams that deliver products and services in direct support of the strategy.

However, for larger organizations, it will be appropriate to distinguish business units that are associated with distinct strategic drivers. Strategy formulation will have provided the clues to possible business units by answering some basic strategic questions:

- How does the enterprise's business model break down its value chain(s)?

- What are the products/services the enterprise delivers to each customer group?

- How might the customer base be segmented into distinct populations?

Your answers to these questions should allow you to identify potential strategic business units. Strategic business units are not independent businesses within a corporate conglomerate concept. We are assuming that the enterprise as a whole shares some common strategic elements or core competencies – identity – but business units are a way of breaking the business down into more manageable, strategically related groups that add measurable value as part of the strategy. Business units might be distinguished by value-chain steps or by geographic location. They might be distinguished by the maturity stage of their products or services, or even by some commonality of their customers. Business units might be distinguished by some combination of product lifecycle stage, customers, or geographic location.

With the caveat that virtually every industry has its own value-chain distinctions, and that value-chain designed business units are only one example, consider the following conceptual example: A company that pursues a technology-leader strategy as their overarching competitive advantage within an industrial or service industry setting has a leadership group that values functional expertise. Using the value-chain concept to establish business units, the organizational structure might look as follows:

- The first business unit might be the *Research* business unit – the purpose of this business unit enterprise is to create value by identifying and establishing a brand identity relationship with potential clients/customers. The depth of the relationship and the purchasing potential of the clients determine the value created. A massive customer list of people who say they "know the brand" is of lowest value; buyers who say "our brand is their best solution" and have large revenue booking potential are of the highest value.

- These potential clients may be purchased by the next value chain business unit – *Acquire*. This business unit makes the deal happen with first-time clients. The value they add depends on the sales price and conditions of service required.

- A production or operating business unit – *Retain* – might buy these new customers and actually provide the product or service as well as be responsible for secondary and follow-up sales. The value they add is associated with cost of service and additional business generated.

- If the company has other strategically related, but distinct, business lines, a fourth business unit – *Extent* – might provide an entirely different service or product to these customers (think hardware as the first product and applications consulting as the second business line).

Depending on size, these business units might be served by common support businesses (finance, accounting, human resources, etc.), or have internal-support business teams.

You may be thinking that the above description of a business unit breakdown sounds like a functional organization with different names – marketing, sales, operations, etc. It could be, and yet it is *not*. The names do describe part of their purpose, but it is key in this relational model to define and then manage every activity within a business model concept by asking questions like the following: What is the business purpose of the unit? How do these functions add value? How could you measure it? The business unit breakdown could have been around geography rather than functions, in which case the concepts of *research, acquire, retain,* and *extent* could all be done within a business unit covering a strategically defined geographic area (i.e., central Scotland). Remember, the business unit organizational level is primarily a way of breaking down the organization into manageable units, using a distinct, measurable, strategy related, business purpose to define the units.

Once the top level of the organizational unit has been defined by its business purpose, the next step is to disaggregate these high-level business units into smaller and smaller product, service or support business teams until you arrive at the individual, Me Inc. business unit. At each level of disaggregation, each team must be defined by their business purpose (again, their customers and products or services) and how they add value. Whatever the process you choose, always make sure that each business unit's and business team's purpose clearly links to strategy.

The Business Teams

Whether it describes the entire enterprise or only one strategic element of the business, the business unit has a strategic-level job to do. Business teams are integrated within the business unit and are the workhorses for getting this strategic job done. These business teams are the pieces that make the whole, and yet they are complete businesses in their own right. That is, you need to remember that, conceptually, every successive team, group, etc. right down to Me Inc. is a whole business. Each is an integrated, business-purpose defined *internal enterprise,* connected by their individual identities (strategies) to the overall identity (strategy) of the larger enterprise.

The leaders of each business team form the leadership team for the business unit. Individually they and their team are accountable for the performance of their own business, and collectively, they are responsible for the performance of the whole business unit. We will speak a bit more about this when we discuss *Team Leader Teams* later in *Chapter 10*.

To arrive at what constitutes the business teams within units, we unbundle the business unit products and services into their distinct components. Every enterprise is unique, and thus the best supporting structure of business teams will be unique to the enterprises' circumstance. However, this should not be an excuse to maintain politically sensitive (sacred cow) structures that do not represent strategic focus and/or allow for clearly definable business-purpose groupings. Following are some common types of business teams:

1. **Customer Solutions Teams** – the people responsible for product/service development from concept to launch. These teams might be called "business development" in some enterprises. They include product design, research and development, market research, and etc.

2. **Material Conversion Teams** – the people who turn raw materials into finished products or services. In manufacturing, these are the operations teams, and in a service business, these are the teams that deliver the service to the customer, converting their skills and knowledge into customer-valued services.

3. **Support Services Teams** – the people (either internal or external) who provide services or support products for other teams. Such teams might include the accounting teams doing payables and receivables, or the human resource administration teams.

4. **Technical Services Teams** – the people who provide the technical specialization to the other teams. Such teams might include digital technology or industry technical specialists who might work within internal consulting boutiques.

5. **Transaction Processing Teams** – the people doing sales, order taking, and scheduling raw material ordering through product or service delivery.

6. **Corporate Risk Teams** – the people responsible for strategy development in the areas of planning, law, insurance, labor/ personnel, finance, assurance, public relations, information systems, and etc. Now, you might be saying, "Oh, you mean traditional staff functions." Not exactly. We mean only that part of these functions that involves the development of the strategic and tactical approach. The implementation (trans-actional) activities for much of these functions are services. For example, much of traditional human resource work is administrative services, while the policy piece is a risk man-agement issue.

Obviously, this breakdown is not comprehensive, but these are ideas for how you might think about the business team concept design. One point of this breakdown is the introduction of terminology that can cause staff to describe their tasks from a different perspective. New descriptions are not just cute names for old functions – they can provide a new perspective on how the teams fit into the big picture. For example, a material conversion team using bricks to construct a cathedral will hold different possibilities for themselves than a group of brick-masons merely building walls.

After satisfying the strategic realignment requirement by restructuring, the key driver for the business team structure is the ability to identify products and customers for each team. This step allows you to use mar-kets to guide each organizational group. Adherence to the *Competition Sets the Standards* law is difficult, if not impossible, without some form of market definition.

It is quite probable that there will be smaller groups of internal enter-prises within these business teams, and even teams within those smaller teams. Although every organization can be flattened by using internal market processes as *managers*, the idea here is not to flatten the organi-zation but to create each internal enterprise as a business. This market environment supplants traditional management control. Responsibility becomes a demand of the markets rather than of the leadership.

Chapter 10

Coming together is a beginning. Keeping together is progress.
Working together is success.
Henry Ford

Living Within the Structural Frame

The business unit and business team structural framework is necessary to support the Relational Management Model. If the structural re-jigging for the organization is minor, then it is time to start working with individuals from the Me Inc. concept – focusing on identity and using the leadership practices discussed in Section I. If the structural changes are more substantial, then you may be looking at re-staffing each team. In either case, it will be useful to look at leadership processes necessary to this business-purpose team structure. The purpose of this chapter is to present relational methodology for managing this structural framework.

Team Staffing

The organizational structure of business-purpose teams linked to strategy must consist of Me Inc. building blocks. Teams need more than purpose and goals for success. They require complementary skill sets – complementary professional skills (technical, administrative, etc.) and complementary interpersonal skills – as defined by their business purpose. Staffing to fill these required skill sets without overloading the teams with bodies requires abandoning the position concept and accepting the core team and extended team member concept.

In an organization accustomed to position grading based on the number of people supervised and/or a culture of hierarchical control of positions, team leaders will require coaching when designing the staffing for these teams. It is important to note that a business team requiring well-rounded skills (such as technical, marketing and sales abilities, analytical talent, people skills, etc.) does *not* need to have one person for each required function or skill. Some team members may contribute more than one of the required skills to the team's skill set. The demand for some skill requirements may vary over time and can be filled either by part-time players or hired on an on-demand activity basis. The important issue is to get the team thinking about their work responsibilities from the broader perspective of a business, of the breadth of skill required to deliver business results rather than to do jobs.

The need for collaboration between teams (the collaboration is agreement among team leaders to allow individuals on multiple teams) and the lack of well-defined Me Inc. résumés can further complicate staffing in the beginning. Expect this process to be messy, requiring some amount of *shaking out*. As the organization gets used to contribution defining relationships, and as leadership practices evolve to reinforce collaboration, the organization will improve its ability to deal with staffing issues. In the interim, while the organization is in the process of maturing sufficiently, use the following tools to manage business team staffing issues:

1. **Business Team Size**: Let competition set the standards to help team leaders size their internal enterprise (business-team). Performance on the basis of competitive cost for delivery of their services or products will be the key criteria for challenging the number of staff required to deliver the services from each business-team. Since compensation is also competitively set, managing team size is the leader's primary lever for dealing with this issue.

2. **Multiple Team Membership**: Require specialists to work on multiple teams or on a consultancy basis (either as internal- or external-based consultants). Team members who work on more than one team or are from an outside enterprise often

serve as a source of knowledge transfer for an organization. Both the teams and the individuals will benefit from this arrangement.

3. **Team Leader Teams**: Use team-based leadership groups and base team leaders' primary performance measures and their compensation on the performance of their collective group of teams (i.e., business unit) rather than on the performance of the team they lead. This raises their decision-making to the next higher organizational level and encourages collaboration between team leaders. Staffing collaboration will happen when they understand that their accountability is for the performance of the larger team rather than just their individual team.

4. **Human Resource Systems**: Transform the human resource systems (grading, compensation, training, etc.) from position and time-in-service driven to competency/performance-based. Many organizations say that they use competency-based systems, but they are actually using time-in-grade standards or training programs completed to define competency. Build grading, compensation, and training on a solid, competency-based *professional ladder scheme* to bring the human resource system in line with competency principles.

Business Team Size

Although the business-purpose team concept requires every piece of an organization to define themselves as a business rather than an activity, its application is often seen as a break-up of functional departments. The traditional thought is that functional specialization reduces the numbers within an organization. "If we split the functions, it will increase numbers" is a usual statement. Or "How will we decide how big the teams should be?" Both comments come from a command-and-control paradigm of leadership, wherein leaders perceive that controlling numbers and making decisions is their role.

The key leadership issue in deciding team size is to clarify the products and services the team delivers (remember that products are different and distinct from the activities the group performs). If business teams are developed around existing activities and existing job titles, this may not happen as the process may be looking backward instead of forward.

One of our jobs required that we take a look at an accounts payable function. There were 14 people employed to check invoices against service orders. What was their product? After studying the results of the activity, it was clear that there was no product – maybe providing the authorizing persons with assurance, confidence, trust? You see, it turns out that 98% of the invoices were correct, and of those in error, 50% of the errors favored the company. So, 14 people were employed to check correct invoices. The question should not have been, "How many people do we require?" The question should have been, "What is the service being delivered and how will we measure its competitive performance standard?"

Decisions on staffing should be the responsibility of the business team through its team leader. The necessary control is exercised via business accountability through the accountability system. As long as the accountability system is capable of measuring performance from several aspects (i.e., cost, quality, long-term value, safety, customer satisfaction, etc.), decisions on resource requirements should be made at the business team level where responsibility can be matched with accountability. What are the standards set by competition with regard to the size of the business team? Let the team leaders demonstrate that their business is competitive – keep them responsible.

However, focusing on the purpose and products of the teams may still leave a more strategic question unanswered. For industries requiring a high level of technical skills, there is often a need for in-house development of these technical skills. The strategic questions may be as follows: "How can we maintain functional skills and promote cross-team learning and skills transfer in a business team environment?" These questions can be addressed by establishing business teams for each functional skill. The business of each functional business team is to sell functional consulting services as a virtual consulting organization. This internal consulting business can even be managed by an internal business board consisting of team leaders who are its clients. As long as these business board members are held accountable (not allowed to just sit in judgment) for the business performance of the consulting organization, this will ensure that maintaining high quality functional skills is everyone's business.

Multiple Team Membership

A structure organized around contribution allows individuals to be members of more than one team. Business Unit Leaders are members of the Leadership Team as well as the leader of their Business Unit Team. Team Leaders are members of both the Extended Management Team and a Business Unit Leadership Team, as well as the leaders of their specific teams. Functional Teams will be made up of highly experienced functional experts who may also be individual contributors within a Business Team.

Within the ranks of the individual contributors, specialists may be assigned to provide their support to two, three, or more teams – each relationship based upon their contribution to that team. These individuals will have a stronger sense of their Me Inc. than individuals assigned to only one team, as the contribution from these specialists will be more easily identified and specified.

No organization ends at the boundaries of its organizational chart, be it a single team or a multinational corporation. Every organization can be thought of as concentric circles, with each layer having a different type of contribution-defined relationship. An individual may be a core team member of one team and an extended team member of another, or even suppliers from outside of the organization can be members of the Team Community as shown in the visual on page 141.

> *As an example of this multiple team concept, a software programmer with contributions of discernment and linking skills might be a member of the IT Business Systems Team as well as be a member of the Financial Services Support Team. This programmer's Me Inc. business is selling physical and financial data as information for customers' control processes. The relationship to the IT Team is based on the application of standards to ensure enterprise-wide system integrity and compatibility. The relationship to the Financial Team is based upon the delivery of special reports to address unique control problems. This person is much more than a software designer who writes code according to the specifications of the customer, but an enterprise that looks to the purpose of the information requirement and links the data with the user while finding ways to ensure that system standards are not compromised. In other words, this individual provides software system solutions that connect their customer with the information needed to realize their business purpose.*

In other words, Me Inc. can be a part of several teams. In reality, even core team members will often serve on other temporary teams or be a part of a professional community within or outside of their enterprise. This multiple client concept is a relational reality that is in tension with fixed organizational structures. Relationships Defined by Contribution work to eliminate this tension.

Team Leader Teams

Working within a relational model, you will form each level of management into a leadership team with an identified business purpose and accountability, and you will hold these teams accountable for the performance of the larger enterprise as well as for the performance of their own specific team. To use carrot-and-stick language and boil it down to money terms: a team leader's performance compensation is based first on the performance of the larger team. If that performance meets standards, then and only then is the performance of their specific team considered

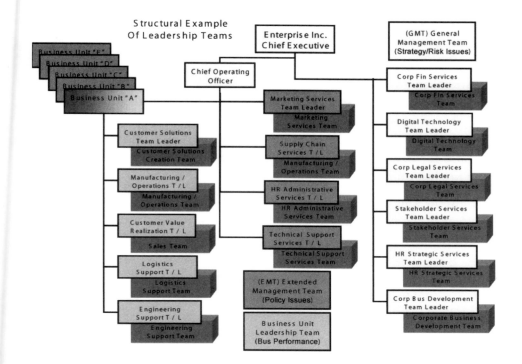

Structural Example Of Leadership Teams

in the compensation equation. You might also base at least 50% of the individual team leader's accountability on performance of the larger group. We participated in one business where the individual's accountability was based 100% on the collective performance of the whole group of team leaders. Now, that really made for teamwork amongst these leaders.

This higher level accountability of the leadership team will raise the conversation of the team leaders to the next organizational level and compel collaboration. With this higher level accountability present, each team leader must make decisions based upon the greater good for the larger team before considering the value to their individual team. This level of collaboration binds the organization together with linked business objectives and overcomes the problem of business teams declaring independence from the federation that sponsors them. This is a particularly effective way to develop and implement enterprise-wide processes or policies – you hold the broader team accountable for their development and implementation.

The visual above shows groups of team leaders that are designated as business teams, such as the General Management Team, whose business purpose is to manage strategy and risk issues. Other Leadership Teams are Business Unit "A" Leadership Team, whose purpose is the business performance of Unit "A," and the Extended Management Team, whose business purpose is to recommend and manage policy issues across the entire business.

Business team leader teams can also be given accountability for the development of functional expertise as part of an enterprise's core competencies. This overcomes business team leaders' attempt to *employ* only fully trained specialist consultants on their team, leaving the enterprise with no place for new graduates to gain the practical experience needed for their Me Inc. and for the organization.

The interlocking of the organization through these leadership teams is a key to ensuring cross-business collaboration. The idea of utilizing an extended management team to address cross-business issues not only places these developing leaders in a position of broad business responsibility but is an excellent way to give them experience as general managers. Since they are responsible for cross-business policy, they must own it during implementation within their own business. Having a voice in policy makes each team leader take responsibility for the impact of their actions on others. There will be no more *them and us* with regard to the senior leadership team and the next level within the organization.

Human Resource Systems

Me Inc. does not fit easily into traditional human resource systems, which are often designed by looking at where the organization has been (e.g., position descriptions based on what activities the person in this job performs) and/or to ensure that everyone is treated equally (e.g., time-based compensation – even if this only means *annual* raises). As the organization transitions from command-and-control, your Human Resources department must lead the way into this Relational Management Model by transforming their systems to allow for acknowledgement of individual purpose, identity and accountability. This requires a competency/performance-based approach for all human resource systems.

The first step in this process is to use individual identities defined by contribution as the sort key when filling positions. For example, basic interviewing processes would center on the three relational elements with the objective of understanding the person's Me Inc. identity statement. The résumé's portfolio of accomplishments would be supplemented with a summary of contributions. As a means to fill positions, the "right contribution for the right situation" is a refreshing change from "past experience for future challenges." As a second step, during the hiring process all applicants might be required to write a purpose statement. Then, documentation to accompany an intra-company transfer might include revision of this purpose statement to encompass the business purpose of their new team.

It is increasingly obvious that the traditional position grading process is falling victim to the rapid pace of change in work processes today. By the time an enterprise-wide grading exercise can be completed, 20 percent of the positions are obsolete. The obvious replacement within a relational model is a professional ladder scheme that is entirely aligned with Me Inc., which measures demonstrated skills and knowledge in combination with the individual's identity statement. In its fullest form, this system will allow individuals to see themselves not as a position or even a profession or trade, but rather, as an identity-based business.

I once was a "Suit." Now I am "Me Inc.!"

Position or job descriptions themselves also must change. Because they are based around the identity necessary to deliver the required contribution, relational management gives positions a personality of sorts. The job description should not be based upon the activities involved but defined by the contribution the job makes to the overall enterprise and thus the attributes of the person who might fill the position. It is much more of a challenge to describe what a position is expected to contribute rather than to construct a list of what it does. However, one test of a position's performance connection is the ability of the Human Recourses department to describe the *job's* contribution as it links to the performance vision of the organization.

Because performance requirements get increasingly more demanding over time, it makes little sense to use either to-do lists or experience as the basis for position descriptions or personnel selection. Defining position contribution brings organizations closer to linking personal identity with positions, a possibility that will revolutionize the search for talent.

The traditional process of evaluating individuals to look for weaknesses is also subject to challenge under the Relational Management Model. When the process is centered on identity, developmental growth will be pursued from an understanding of the strengths and identity of the individual. This will challenge both traditional performance evaluations and training concepts designed to identify and improve upon weaknesses. It is well proven that it takes far less effort to improve performance when training is based upon an individual's strengths rather than on correcting weaknesses.

Bending the Structure

This entrepreneurial, business team, structural model is a way of managing interfaces within the enterprise – a way of managing that moves beyond a lines-and-boxes organizational structure. Relationships defined by contribution provide structural flexibility without diminishing accountability and clarity. Interfaces defined by contribution soften the hard lines of organizational structure, focusing both internal and external groups and individuals on performance rather than territory.

Internally, for example, the Human Resources team can be defined by its contribution as a provider of skills (either through its training, relationship with external providers of skilled workers, or employment services), or Human Resources can be defined by its contribution to cost control for managing salary grades and compensation. The interface relationships will be decidedly different depending on which contribution definition is used. Externally, you might define an engineering partnership by its contribution toward common performance measures, or you can design the relationship around a contractual payment schedule. The engineering firm's relationship is then either a contribution to the performance of the business or as a time-and-material based contractor.

We are not suggesting an end to traditional business arrangements. Contractors still require contracts, and managing human resources is still a specialized function within any organization of approximately 50 or more people. However, the relationship should be defined according to the contribution required for success rather than dealing with internal (or for that matter external) conflicts through structural realignment. For example, if you define and measure the contribution from procurement as cost savings, you can be assured of continuing conflict with the operations team. They will see contribution from procured resources in far broader terms – timeliness and lifecycle performance to name just two. In an "I don't report to you" environment, this means constant management interventions to keep things running smoothly. In a contribution-based relationship between the parties, however, the need for these interventions is eliminated.

The need for organizational charts may never go away; but when you allow contribution to define the relationship, structure's control component *can be aligned* to the performance commitments of the organization. In an emergency, there will be a need for the classic command-and-control structure (X reports to Y) to come to the forefront and "direct the traffic." In a crisis, the performance commitment may be defined as the prevention of physical or fiscal loss, whereby control is the dominant contribution needed. When the crisis passes, however, the contribution required from "Control" subsides and other, more critical, contributions redefine relationships within the organization.

For most organizations, if participants in the management processes were not based upon what organizational chart position they occupy but by what they contribute to the performance of the business, there would be a decidedly different approach to determining a meeting attendee list. A place at the table would be determined by contribution, but more importantly, the organization would have achieved a more flexible way to deal with structure.

Call Me Accountable and I Am

A s stated early in this discussion, every one of us *likes* to know that we are meeting the expectations of our job. To be accountable in any relationship, we *need* to know we are meeting expectations. Accountability is essential to ensure relational responsibility by setting the hands in motion, connecting the head and the heart to action. *Competition Sets the Standards,* but without some method of calibration, perception and reality quickly become distant relatives. In this section we will look at how accountability gets addressed within our Relational Management Model. We call this last element of the model:

- **A Strategy-Linked and Cascaded Accountability System,** which supplies tangible goals and creates the assurance framework to allow the elimination of command-and-control style procedures. The market-driven internal environment created by the business-purpose team structure allows for meaningful **accountability** measurement instead of authoritarian judgments as the basis for control. Linked and cascaded measures keep the organization connected to its strategic foundation.

Nearly everyone claims to have this form of accountability system, but few are actually working within the context of the relational model. There are two key differences if your accountability system is to work within the relational model:

1. The relational model approaches accountability from an individual responsibility perspective. Trust and honesty are assumed, but it is each individual's responsibility to ensure that such trust continues to be justified. When failure occurs, the individual(s) involved (if they are still employed) start back at step one on the trust ladder, but the entire system does not get revamped to avoid future individual failure.

2. The other difference is in directional focus. Accountability within the relational model operates within the present and future domains – not the past. What is current performance and what are we going to do about improving it? Performance expectations have either been met or they have not. No story about *why* is required, but rather, what actions are required now.

Even though accountability is more than just a system – it is a way of being – organizations need a system to support this way of being. Although a system by itself cannot deliver a way of being, an accountability system will deliver responsibility and performance when it:

-   Recognizes that performance is a relative term defined by what competitors are delivering versus what the organization is delivering for its stakeholders

-   Minimizes, or eliminates, the use of judgment for evaluating performance. It is not the boss who sets performance standards, which are instead competitively defined and competitively measured

-   Links the organization to the strategy of the enterprise and drives collaboration horizontally across the business

-   Reflects enterprise values or governance issues as well as hard outcomes

As you read through this section, please keep one key thought in mind. If you measure something, that something will get people's attention and action. If you measure the right things, the right actions will follow. If you measure the wrong things, wrong actions will follow.

Chapter 11

All things are difficult before they are easy.
Thomas Fuller

The Accountability System

D efining the path for organizational direction is not just the act of developing a *Strategy*. It is also linking the organization to this *Strategy* and continuously adjusting that linkage to keep the enterprise on course (as either strategic assumptions are tweaked or environmental corrections are required). The Accountability System is the tool that communicates these strategic tactics and adjustments due to the environmental scanning process. One year, the accountability system's focus may be on quality, the next year on cost, and the next year on innovation. This is a critical connecting process that translates strategic design into action. We all know that *strategy formulation* is not the real business problem – *strategy implementation* is the difficult problem for managers. The *Strategy-linked and Cascaded Accountability System* overcomes this implementation problem by delivering two critical pieces of organizational connectedness:

- It *brings the Strategy to life* through cascaded metrics, translating strategy into operational terms.

- It *provides assurance and control* through a comprehensive set of metrics designed to balance various performance and risk perspectives.

Measurement is a language form for clarifying strategic concepts. What gets measured is what the organization says is important, and what gets rewarded is what the organization really values, but the accountability system comes before the compensation system, so we'll save that discussion for the compensation perspective in *Chapter 14.* The accountability system can be designed to speak the Strategy to the organization, by targeting, measuring, and reporting on activities that are critical to the organization's Strategic Intent. No single metric or single perspective can guide an organization (or any one piece of it) – balance with some tension between metrics is inevitable and desirable. In fact, to provide strategic assurance and control, the metrics *must* be in tension to address risk management issues that are invariably a part of any strategy.

Accountability metrics must align and connect, as well as guide an organization strategically. This means that they must cause the organization to work together as well as to work for the success of the individual group or team. This element of design is as hard, or harder, than finding strategic insights, but it is equally important. Other elements of relational leadership might be learned or coached, but discovering strategic insights and establishing appropriate metrics requires business experience, strategic comprehension, and awareness of how people make choices.

Defining metrics does not end with the preparation of the initial measuring system (scoreboard, scorecard, or tally sheet – name it what you will). In fact, it is a continuing job. Because the Accountability System provides measurement, this feedback should cause leadership to question strategic issues and highlight internal processes that require attention. The more you learn, the more you will need to adjust the metrics to keep the enterprise focused and aligned.

In this chapter, we will provide the conceptual framework for a *Strategy-Linked and Cascaded Accountability System,* so that you can design your enterprise-specific system.

Prepare a Tally Sheet

The *Tally Sheet* is the place where all the metrics for each organizational level get translated into targets and the outcomes get reported. The *Tally Sheet* for the Accountability System communicates the strategy by measuring what is important, and it is designed to connect the organization horizontally and vertically. The *Tally Sheet* flows from the strategy, measuring both the drivers of the strategy and the expected outcomes. The *Tally Sheet* should allow you to look at the enterprise from several perspectives, ensuring that short-term performance issues are balanced by long-term value creation measures. Customer objectives and organizational capacity development should also be considered, but stay-in-business requirements, like income and revenue drivers, can never be forgotten.

Preparing the metrics for an enterprise *Tally Sheet* is a leadership role, just as developing and continuously updating the strategy is a leadership role. However, you can let go of any need to get these right – the metrics will change with time anyway. Try not to get them wrong, of course, but the point here is that you need to recognize that measurement is an opportunity for learning. Thus, it is unlikely that you will get everything right before you begin this learning process.

Metrics will change as learning occurs and as the strategy navigates the changing environment. Just as leadership must be constantly working on strategic thinking, leadership must also pay attention that the metrics are guiding the organization along its strategic pathway. Metrics can be added, deleted, rested (not used for a period), or altered as needed. The organization's response and competitor or environmental changes should guide leadership's decisions in this regard. Metrics are a behavioral steering device – steering the organization toward its Strategic Intent – so do not be afraid to change the metrics if you get actions that do not drive the organization toward your Living Performance Vision.

In selecting the areas for measurement, *Balance* and *Connectivity* (linkage) are critical ingredients.

- *Balance* to ensure that equal consideration is given to seemingly conflicting requirements (e.g., quality and low cost, safety and efficient performance, or short-term and long-term impacts).

- *Connectivity* to ensure that everyone is able to understand how their actions influence the overall strategy of the enterprise.

One of the earliest published accountability systems was the Balanced Scorecard[1] process. When this system was first designed, *Balance* was addressed, in part, by considering four perspectives:

- Customers
- Internal Processes
- Financial
- Employee Learning and Growth

We often use perspectives that spread financial and process measures, such as:

- Long-term Value Growth
- Current Operations
- Customers
- Employees

Either approach to the four perspectives might be considered more demonstrative of the need to measure from a variety of perspectives than as prescriptive requirements. If these perspectives do not feel right for your enterprise, develop perspectives that are more meaningful for your enterprise's environment – but of course ensure that all your key strategic perspectives are reflected. If these are a good start, consider how they can be represented by metrics.

The *Long-term Value Growth* perspective requires that you look behind the numbers, as these are often based upon assumptions driven by current business conditions: price, volume, cost, etc. Determining the source of the value change will often indicate how well the strategy is working and where to focus attention. If the value change is due to price assumptions, this may be something the organization has little control over and thus your focus must be on competitive cost positioning as the strategic driver. If the value change is due to technological advancements put in place by your organization, this may indicate that this strategic driver is working well.

The *Current Operations* perspective is often used to address product safety and environmental performance as well as cost and productivity. The performance of internal processes, such as product design, can also fall within this perspective. Customer retention or measures of time required for customer service are often covered under the *Customer* perspective, as both can be strategic indicators.

The *Employee* perspective should not be confused with an employee attitude survey, although surveys can be used to measure how well these stakeholders are connected to the Living Performance Vision. Employee growth and learning certainly fall within this perspective. An often used, but personally objectionable, metric is the number of average training days – our experience demonstrates little correlation between training and learning or performance growth. An innovation measure (number of new programs, products, technologies, etc.) to access employee performance contribution holds more appeal for us, but only if connected to a strategy based on innovation. Another indicator that is often used is employee turnover rate, especially if the strategy assumes a relational service delivery model.

Balance and connectivity are both addressed by looking for *leading* and not just *trailing* measures of both performance and strategic success. Most financial measures (income, expenditures or cost, ROI, etc.) are by definition trailing measures for they produce a picture of what has already occurred. Market share growth, customer contacts (e.g., web site hits), project proposal submissions, or patents awarded and pending (technology leader strategy) may be leading measures or drivers critical to strategic success.

Obviously, because metrics are a reflection of strategy, the choice of metrics is unique to each enterprise. However, it is important to note that it is easy to overwhelm the organization with a large number of metrics. To get balance and connectivity, and to cover the four perspectives, will require a minimum of eight measures. If you find your organization moving beyond sixteen at each organizational level, there may be a distinct lack of strategic focus developing. A plethora of high-level measures may even be a sign that the accountability system is part of a micromanagement culture rather than a strategy-linked process. This micro focus may not allow enough *Space* for creativity to emerge or for accountability.

The most effective method for developing a *Tally Sheet* is to use a cross-organization project team led by one senior executive. This has the benefit of inclusion and allows for the training of future leaders for the development of subsequent Tally Sheets for each organizational level as the accountability system is cascaded.

This accountability project team's first task is to define the enterprise-level perspectives and associated metrics. They do this by analyzing the existing strategy to identify its underlying assumptions and drivers – linking the products and contribution of the enterprise to its customers; and by facilitating leadership team workshops to agree the resulting enterprise-level metrics. Once identified, these top-level measures define the collective accountability of the leadership team.

The next step is to cascade the metrics down and across the organization. This is not a simple case of dividing the metrics. In fact, this step should not even be approached as a dividing or divvying-up process. The top-level metrics are related to the strategy, or unique identity, of the organization, and likewise, each subsequent cascade of metrics should also relate to the business-purpose of each business unit, asset team, business team, work group, etc. Yes, they must be connected to the enterprise-wide strategy. Yes, some of the metrics, especially with regard to the Employee perspective may even be the same, but each team's metrics should also be specific to the identity (strategy) of their work. In addition, cross-enterprise initiatives (support for the strategy) must be emphasized with the use of *common* metrics for business teams and service/support teams.

Cascade the Metrics

The top-level, enterprise-wide metrics should guide the cascading process, as it is critical to achieve connectivity between Business Inc. and Me Inc. The cascading process mirrors the organizational structure, meaning that each team, unit, group will have metrics that hold them accountable for their contribution to the organization as a whole. If your organizational structure is such that you have different levels of management groups, such as an extended management team or a functional management team, then each of these teams must also have its contribution measured as part of the accountability system. It is often at the level of these management teams that accountability for cross-business initiatives and processes occurs (see *Team Leader Teams* in *Chapter 10*). As an example, accountability for an enterprise-wide strategic procurement initiative is not held by the procurement manager, but rather, by the management team for which procurement provides services.

The cascading process is an excellent opportunity for teams to re-confirm their business purpose and their relationship with the enterprise-wide strategy. Using team members from the original enterprise-wide metric development project team to lead these cascading workshops links each team with the original, top-level work. It also requires the teams to answer that ultra-critical question: "How does our work support the

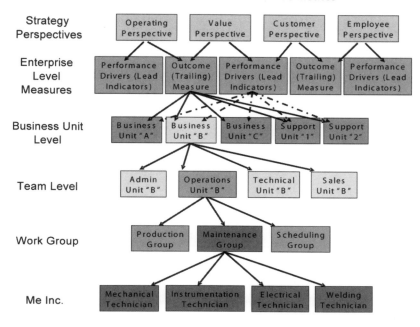

Cascaded Performance Metrics

enterprise strategy?" Then, they can begin to answer what is perhaps the next most critical question: "How should our contribution(s) be measured?"

Establishing well linked metrics becomes successively more difficult as the process cascades; and without leadership attention, it can degenerate into a mechanical, fill-in the forms, objective-setting process. At the Me Inc. level, this metric setting accountability replaces (transforms) the personnel evaluation or appraisal process. It is also important to begin the Me Inc. transformation from the beginning of an individual's tenure with your organization and to ensure that all interactions with the organization take place from this same accountability perspective, so bring the Human Resources group onboard the initial organization-wide metrics setting effort to allow them to integrate this perspective into their systems.

Keeping Me Inc. connected through their cascaded metrics gives the accountability system real performance traction. The performance conversation then has real meaning for the individual – purpose and identity are linked with accountability. Integrating the cascaded, individual metrics with the human resource systems also brings the strategy to life for the individual, because they can see how organizational processes connect and support strategy. You will hear no more of this: "They tell me to do these things, and then HR comes along and puts me on a training course for something else!"

It is important to ensure that the enterprise's strategy is the context for every team workshop and Me Inc. cascade conversation. We often open workshops with a strategy presentation, and then we encourage a discussion of this information's relevance to the team. How does the team's business-purpose support this strategy? Why is their work important? What or who is their competition? These are some of the questions that will provide the context and make the link from team to enterprise strategy.

We suggest you use self-teaching procedures, allowing the group to identify possible metrics rather than telling them what the consultants recommend. Incorporate a process of challenge into the work, so that the team must answer a number of questions about their recommended metrics. The key question to ask, of course, is the requirement to specify how the metrics support the organization's *strategy*: "How might our customers judge us as successful?" It is also important to be clear about the measurement process for each metric. And, then in preparation for the next steps, you can ask, "How will you establish a competitively justified target?" As they answer these questions, team members will begin to see the *strategy* as part of their work.

Some metrics must be a part of the big-picture strategic story, and some should address the individual team strategy. It is great if one metric can do both – an enterprise strategy focusing on geographic growth will have metrics about new customers, while the business development team may have metrics about new distribution arrangements. The metrics thus designed will be consistent in strategic focus but unique to the organizational level. Remember: the organization is strategically linked as the strategic concept is cascaded even though the specific metric is not.

As the cascade takes place, continue to check that metrics are not being duplicated, like measuring things that are well correlated. For example, operating income and cash flow may or may not tell a different strategic story. Consider whether each is contributing something of value for organizational or team emphasis. Also, it is particularly important that business teams as well as service and support teams establish metrics to share the responsibility for each others' success. That is, each team must have some metric that holds them responsible for the success of other teams upon which they depend or vice versa.

As the strategy adjusts to external environmental change, it is likely that individual team metrics, and perhaps the enterprise-wide metrics, will change. This should not happen each quarter, but some change each year is quite possible. The astute use of metrics guides the organization strategically, and by changing the metric mix, different elements of the strategy can be emphasized. As the strategy formulation process creates new insights, defines some element more clearly, or recognizes a need to improve some element of performance, leaders signal new insights by altering the metrics to focus on different aspects of the business. If the basic strategic thinking is sound, this should not be a 90-degree swing in direction, but more like a mild course correction or realignment.

Establishing the first set of comprehensive, cascaded metrics is a major step toward ensuring the successful implementation of your strategy, and just being able to describe the strategy in measurable terms introduces clarity for everyone. If you went no further (and obviously we are not recommending this), the clarity achieved at this step would probably pay for the time and effort spent. Now, however, we will turn to putting this clarity to work.

Note

1. *The Balanced Scorecard by Robert S. Kaplan and David P. Norton, Harvard Business School Publishing (1996). We believe this concept is based in part on an accountability process implemented by a North Sea marine service contractor during the time that the initial Performance Connection processes were used to transform the oil and gas industry in the North Sea.*

Chapter 12

In modern business it is not the crook who is to be feared most, it is the honest man who doesn't know what he is doing.
William Wordsworth

Implementing the Accountability System

We have intentionally separated our discussion of the implementation of the Accountability System from the design of the metrics. One reason is to reduce the tension that develops the closer the organization gets to setting targets and measuring performance. It seems that people are a little more relaxed as they discuss what should be measured (metrics) when the level of performance (the target) is not present.

Although setting the metrics for each team is a big job, the work does not end there. However, the level of executive involvement can be somewhat reduced for the next step. Because the metrics give voice to the strategy and measure the contribution of each piece of the organization, executive leadership is essential, but the next step, defining the data sources and codifying the definitions, can be more of a staff support role.

This chapter takes implementation from metric definition through measurement and reporting, including the establishment of targets. We will start the process of formalizing the metrics by drafting a chart-of-accounts to ensure consistency, and thereby, to ensure the integrity of the system.

Define the Metric and Source

Although it is highly probable that many of the metrics were developed with an eye to the source of the data, some of the metrics may be more conceptual (i.e., what is the market that is being measured?). It is now necessary to do some detail work and formalize the system. We recommend starting the definition process by reviewing the source of the data, a first step that avoids overcomplicating the system and makes it simpler to collect data. *It is of little value to design some complex definitional basis and data collection process that is either time or cost prohibitive to implement.* Even in this day and age of electronic data collection and sorting, the KISS (Keep It Short and Simple) rule is valuable.

The financial (trailing) measures may be the easiest to undertake in this step because they are probably already being measured and have financial chart-of-account definitions. Of course, certifiable financial accounting data may differ from managerial accounting data, and it is probable that the more useful cost data will be of the managerial variety. The *Tally Sheet* must speak the language of strategy, which is not necessarily the language of the balance sheet, income statement, or asset register.

As the language of strategy is often a bit conceptual, the definitions for the *Tally Sheet* metrics may require some informed judgment to get the metrics 80% accurate with 20% of the effort. Remember that relative consistency in reporting is more valuable than absolute accuracy. As recent accounting scandals demonstrate, accuracy in reporting is a very illusive thing and may not be worth the effort required. Timeliness in reporting is also more important than absolute accuracy. We look for measures that can be reported within 7 to 10 working days after the close of a quarterly reporting period. If the reporting period is shorter, the lag time in reporting may be shorter as well, and conversely, if the reporting time is longer, the lag time in reporting may be longer.

As the *Tally Sheet* process is in part about behavior guidance, it is helpful to think about it as follows: Even within the relational model, some people may try to make themselves look good by manipulating accountability reporting by arguing definitional intricacies. When that occurs, you have your demonstration of behavior. If trying to look good is your desired behavior, great. If not, the behavior has been exposed and you can now deal with it as a relationship issue.

Leadership must determine if the metrics drive the desired behaviors. Obviously, it is the result (i.e., behavior and learning) that is important, not the metric. The metric should be changed if the desired behavior does not occur or if the strategic assumption changes. Do not be afraid to try a metric and then to change it as learning takes place, but do think through the logic of what you propose to measure.

> *We recall a situation where more focus on operational safety was needed. The organization decided to initiate a near-miss reporting system — to measure what precedes an accident in order to get people to be more aware of safety problems. The idea was to be aware of unsafe acts before they resulted in an accident — a good idea. However, the system was implemented in the absence of any accountability system — people were encouraged to report but not required to take any responsibility for altering the work processes. Corrective action was seen as a leadership responsibility. The people reporting the near-misses were only measured on the number reported — the higher the better. In no time at all, the head office was flooded with near-miss reports — hundreds upon hundreds of them — so many that the organization could not respond to any of the recommendations and cynicism regarding the system was the most prominent behavioral change.*

Start with the things that can be easily captured, and integrate the metrics capture with as many existing systems as possible. For example, if the investment approval process requires some form of Net Present Value (NPV) analysis, use this as the source of the Value Creation metric. At the team level, use self-reporting techniques until a more systematic arrangement can be made. Clarify that self-reporting is subject to spot audit and let the team take responsibility for what they report — trust them and make them responsible for maintaining that trust.

Setting the Targets

Setting the actual targets for each metric is the next step. This is a critical step in the process. The level of buy-in establishes the level of commitment to the targets. The maturity level (dependent, independent, or interdependent) and the risk tolerance characteristics of the team or individual may play a part in the process of target setting. Target setting is an excellent chance for the organization to increase understanding of *Competition Sets the Standards* and to understand the choice-and-consequences element of the leader/subordinate relationship.

The targets must bear some relationship to competitive standards of performance, but because targets are being set for a future period, exact competitive comparisons are not possible – the competitors have not performed the activities yet either so you are taking a snapshot of a moving vehicle. Often you will find the competitive standard is a range, either because exact comparisons are not possible or because competing firms represent a range of competition. Your industry may even require that competitive data gathering be done through a third party, causing a further lag in the timeliness and therefore exactness of the standard. Using the context of the enterprise's strategy, a leader might be required to clarify the final target level or at least guide the team's interpretation of the competitive target range. For example, your strategy may require top quartile performance in one area, mid-range performance in another, and being a leader in a third area.

Competition presents challenges!

In organizations where using competitive standards is a new practice, we have seen cases where the final target just seemed impossible to the team. When this is the case, the team's reaction may be justified due to a macro strategic positioning problem. If that is the case for your organization, return to *Chapter 8,* where we talk about getting the strategy in place.

Now, you may be thinking, my business is too small or too unique for us to be focused on external competitors: We don't really have a lot of competition and controlled growth is our target. We respectfully suggest you might want to think again. Competition is present whether you acknowledge it in your strategy or whether you do not. Competition controls the price you charge, in the form of product substitution if not in direct product competition. Your clients or customers are making some type of value/price trade-off – even if your competition is a "do nothing" choice by them. Monopoly positions do exist in some industries, perhaps due to government regulations or resource scarcities. BUT, in the long-run even these barriers will fall, if the producer does not acknowledge competition from some form of substitution. Niche market positioning might well be a goal of your strategic intent, but please recognize that the life-cycle of niches is getting shorter and shorter as competitors find a way around the existing barriers. Ideas and information are virtually free-flowing today and the rate of change due to competitive pressure continues to accelerate. Beware of thinking that competition does not exist in your business arena – it is out there just waiting for you to pretend it does not exist in your special case!

In organizations with well developed strategic and business planning processes, the teams will have captured enough competitive data to establish business unit targets. These teams can be expected to recommend and justify the specific targets based upon their analysis of what it will take to deliver competitive performance, taking into account the strategic drivers and the moving competitive target issues.

And Challenges drive innovation!

For many internal enterprises, especially service and technical support teams, setting targets is seldom as clear cut. Benchmarking for performance targets, while useful at the macro level, is often not very practical for the security services business team, for example, or even the office services business team.

For these team-level targets, start the search for competitive standards by making (or have the team members make) 3 to 5 phone calls to competitors to get a competitor perspective on the standards of performance. Ask about productivity, quality standards, and pricing. Get the team members to think about market pricing mechanisms for their activities. Just get them into a market conversation. Maybe have them work backward from some macro competitively-set benchmark by asking a question like this one: "What would their performance need to be in order for the greater organization to meet these macro competitive standards?" Just get them to *feel* the pressure of competition as the standard setter – this is a big step in moving away from the leader as judge and into an environment of competitive awareness.

For organizations in a highly dependent state of organizational maturity, a leader's initial role might be more proactive – to the point of setting the initial targets and explaining their linkage to competitive standards. Once the system is started, the practice of a leader setting the targets should end as quickly as possible. Even if these targets are set with an understanding of competitive demands, longer-term use of top-down target setting continues a dependency relationship between a leader and team members.

- The team will be missing an opportunity to learn first hand about their competition and how competition sets their standards of performance.

- The team will be missing a chance to gather new ideas by looking outside of their workplace environment.

- The accountability process will be missing engagement. Engagement of the heart and thus real commitment to targets requires buy-in and acceptance of responsibility for delivery. Without this engagement there is a large risk that team members will view the target as another arbitrary demand and delivery as really the responsibility of whoever sets the target. You will hear statements like, "We will *try* but it is really not our responsibility if things do not go right."

If the leader does the initial target setting, the result might be the initial rejection of the targets and the logic used to justify them, a low level of commitment, and the continuation of dependency thinking as evidenced in statements like, "We will need more training, new equipment, more cooperation from others, etc." These are fear-of-failure reactions, and the team is passing responsibility for meeting the targets back to the leader. Rather than responding to the demands, or providing further justification for the standards, move the conversation into the realm of possibilities: "If you were able to meet these targets, what possibilities might become available?" Help them build possibilities, and help them think of things they might do differently. In addition to helping them identify what they might need to do, acknowledge their concerns and allow that support from the organization is also required. Rather than negotiating the performance standards, turn the conversation toward action – theirs and others as opposed to yours. Give them time to build a non-fear-based relationship with the targets. As they see more possibilities and generate tangible actions, their fears will dissipate.

In short, as quickly as possible, require the team to take responsibility for establishing competitive standards. Ask questions like, "Why is this target being recommended? What is the basis of your judgment? Will this performance level allow the enterprise-wide targets to be met?"

But, you may be asking at this point in our discussion, "What if the target is wrong?" It won't matter. If the metric is right and you measure it, performance will improve but so will the relational IQ of your overall enterprise as regards responsibility, which is what you want to get started. Even if you link this metric to pay, and you are probably thinking about that right now, it doesn't really matter because you are allowed *not* to get it right straight out of the gate. If the improvement provides your organization value, and you return some of that value to the team, you are ahead of the game and on your way to the goal of a relational organization. Just be smart about how you do the linkage to compensation – we say more about that in *Chapter 14* when we provide a compensation framework. For now, let go of getting it right and just let the law of competition get started doing its work raising the performance standard.

It is important to note that we are not saying that relational leadership is a democracy. A leader's commitment is to the success of the overall organization, and thus they have the final say on whether the standards are adequate. The individuals then have a choice of accepting the target or accepting the consequences. The choice to accept the target places the person in a position to be responsible for delivery. The choice to reject the target may have an entirely different consequence. Choice is a wonderful and scary thing. With choice comes responsibility for consequences. Accepting the consequences is called accountability, and that is what this system is about.

If the individual will not accept a minimum standard of performance by declaring his or her responsibility for standards, *leadership can not allow the person to continue to be responsible for that activity*. A commitment to try or a response such as "I will do what you say" is a set-up to fail. Why wait for them to fail? They have made their choice and they are now responsible for the consequences of this action. If business conditions allow leadership to move such an individual to another area where they can agree to meet the performance standards, that is wonderful; but if not, the person has made the choice to end their relationship with the enterprise.

In a dependent internal environment, people are generally risk averse, and getting agreement on competitively-based goals can be a problem; but the opposite can also be true – irresponsibly high goals often get recommended and accepted. Just as the agreement to goals that do not meet competitive standards is irresponsible in that it gives individuals a false sense of performance security, the acceptance of goals that will cause failure and trigger major negative consequences is equally irresponsible. *In setting goals, operate from a commitment to the individuals being successful in their life's work, not just your business activities.*

Measurement and Reporting

The feedback portion of the accountability system is as important as the targets. Performance delivery accelerates as the targets and measurement allow people to know where their performance stands relative to the targets. It is necessary to follow-up with regular measurement and reporting as part of the *Performance Conversation*. How this performance monitoring is handled is a big part of the transformation to *perform-and-learn*. Here is the context for this *Performance Conversation*:

- Relational leadership is not about getting people to work for the approval of leadership. Reporting is not to look good or bad, but to ensure that everyone is aware of where they stand – today's *Start*.

- All conversations are about getting to the future – the *End*. Reviews are to update staff so that decisions about next actions are informed and coordinated.

- Direction is clear. Leadership can then be focused on the support and coaching required.

What is Today's Start? Accountability in a relational context is not about having a third party sit in judgment and report on people's performance. It is not like going into the boss's office and being told what your rating is for the quarter or for the year. The performance standards are understood in advance, and the targets are defined so outcomes are facts and not opinions. "The performance *start* point was here at the beginning of the period; the *start* point today is now moved to here, and the *end* point is still there."

In reality, the bluntness of such a conversation seems just too difficult to enact. We are so conditioned for stories that even the most seasoned accountability performance reporter will find the need to describe a bit of the how and why. If used to describe environmental issues as part of continuous strategic thinking, this is a useful activity, but if the stories slip into excuses, then the direction is backward and a gentle reminder to return to a future focus will be useful.

What are the required actions for getting to the End? The goals are future focused and the performance conversation has a future focus: "What will it now take to get to the target?" Once the current *start* position has been established (where performance stands today), guide the conversation toward the future. Reconfirm the goals that have been established (i.e., provide a tangible definition of future possibilities) and then ask, "What are the actions you plan to take? What support is required of others? How do you plan to access this support? What do you expect from the leadership? Are there any decisions required at this time?" (Notice how the questions keep the participant responsible and do not transfer the responsibility back to the leader.)

Acknowledge the contribution of the individuals and the teams, whatever the performance position. Rest assured that everyone has performed according to their definition of the possibilities presented, and if performance is on track, summarize the strategic learning (links to continuous strategic thinking) from the review. Connect them to the strategy and goals of the larger organization. Schedule the next performance review according to the business cycle (see *Business Management Cycle* in *Chapter 13*). Keep delivering the same amount of *Coaching/Support*.

Adjusting Space. If all is not moving according to performance expectations, leadership must bring some judgment into play. This is not judgment of performance, however, but judgment of the amount of *Space* required to match the competencies of the individual or team and to assess what might be missing for them.

If the performance is above expectation and the team has consistently demonstrated interdependent behaviour, you may consider extending the time between reviews or schedule the next to coincide with some critical decision point. In other words, as a performance track record is established and interdependent behaviour is demonstrated, increase the amount of *Space* available to the team and decrease the Coaching/Support.

If the performance is below expectations and/or the team is demonstrating dependent or independent behaviour, it may be appropriate to reduce the amount of *Space* and determine what is missing for them. Shorten the time between performance conversations, require more reporting on progress, and increase the amount and perhaps type of Coaching/Support. Approach this change in terms of *Space* from a position of support rather than punishment for missing the target. Remember, the point to convey is that it is in everyone's best interest to meet performance expectations and give them all the help they need with this in mind – but leave responsibility for delivery of performance with them.

Tell Me How It Works Together

Before enlightenment: chop wood, draw water.
After enlightenment: chop wood, draw water.
Buddhist proverb.

D aily activities go on within the enterprise amid the aha's of developing strategy and the wonders of experiencing this new relational model. The question before us is how do all these things function together as part of daily business? How do you integrate business processes to bring everything together so that organizational connectedness continues as a normal part of running your business? We will answer these questions in this section.

During transition to this relational model, we worked on the enterprise's vision and on strategy development to produce the road map for the organization. We transformed structure through the introduction of business-purpose defined teams, which brought market forces inside the enterprise's walls, and we introduced an accountability system to connect strategy to daily activities. These were described as singular processes and not regular business cycle events. The need now is to incorporate environmental scanning, planning, and accountability management into everyday business in a seamless sequence of events that do not overload the organization.

Everyone is well aware of how ephemeral, how dream-like, vision and strategic concepts can be once the meetings start, or the phones ring, or budget short-falls occur. However, vision and strategy can only do their work when they are a part of everyday organizational life, and making the vision and strategy live takes a great deal of time and energy. In fact, we cannot afford to let these slip away. There are five parts to continuing the performance connection with the organization:

1. Developing and implementing a "Business Management Cycle" that integrates planning, budgeting, accountability, and decision making.

2. Following the three relational laws when managing all business processes. This includes recognizing that the business-purpose structure must flex as contribution defines the relationships required to keep the strategy ahead of the competition.

3. Using the four leadership practices to teach the organization how to move from their dependency state of being into a collaborative state of interdependence – in other words, keeping people responsible.

4. Continuing environmental scanning and strategic learning as the lead process for maintaining context for the Business Management Cycle; allowing the strategy to migrate the changing external environment.

5. Continuing the process of helping various groups continuously redefine themselves and their contribution to the strategy as their world changes.

The *Business Management Cycle* provides the backbone for maintaining organizational alignment. Environmental scanning and strategic learning provide the context for the alignment work, and the three *Relational Laws* and four *Leadership Practices* build organizational capacity to meet new challenges or to forge positions of strength for the enterprise.

Chapter 13

*The difference between a boss and a leader: a boss says,
'Go!' – a leader says, 'Let's go!'.*
E. M. Kelly

The Business Management Cycle

With the declaration of the enterprise's road map, the big-picture *Direction* has been planned. This is critical context for any actions; but without explicit process, to cause individuals and groups to continually refine the *Living Performance Vision* and *Strategy*, this work will have little impact. Without explicit process, the organization will become disconnected from leadership's vision – the Living Vision transforms into a Dying Vision. Integrating the planning process with the accountability system starts to heal this disconnection.

When it comes to planning, enterprises of fewer than 30 to 50 people might leap directly from high-level *Direction* determinants (*Living Performance Vision* and *Strategy*) to the budgeting process. Often in organizations of this size, the people who define the strategy and vision are the same people who detail the budget. If so, a formal planning process may have little value as a learning and communication tool, and that step in the Planning Cycle might well be skipped. However, once an enterprise exceeds the $3-5 million revenue level, it is time to introduce some formal business planning to link vision and strategy to the annual budgeting process. These business planning activities are the natural starting point for the accountability system. A well-done business plan will identify potential metrics and will establish the ranges for many of the specific performance targets.

As we discussed in the prior section, the accountability system started with the identification of metrics based upon Strategy, and then it was implemented by identifying target performance standards for the metrics, measuring the impact of these metrics, and reporting progress against targets. The Business Management Cycle systematizes this work through regular (i.e., quarterly) performance reviews that integrate planning, control, communications, and authorization. Remember, it is the entire *perform-and-learn* context that makes this systematization powerful. Operated within a command-and-control context, this business cycle will rapidly transition into just another series of time-consuming meetings.

Performance Reviews have the following purpose:

- Clarifying context to ensure strategic alignment of Direction
- Acknowledging progress and contribution toward the targets
- Clarifying Boundaries and adjusting Space
- Coordinating Support/Coaching actions
- Delegating authorities for agreed-upon actions
- Establishing the business context for enterprise communications
- Learning from others within your unit and between organizational units

Under normal business conditions, Performance Reviews might take place quarterly. Quarterly timing allows you to fold in the business planning cycle. However, before moving to the timing cycle for meshing planning and performance reviews, a short overview of the planning process will ensure that we are using common terms.

The Planning Cycle

The Planning Cycle includes everything from the strategic plan to the one-year budget or operating plan. This planning process controls and improves decision making by clarifying options and linking them to the Strategy. Planning does not predict the future and cannot ensure that what is planned will actually come about, however. A request to prepare any one of these plans is a request to learn – in a way; it is a request to be wrong so that learning can take place.

Obviously, a request to be wrong is not to say that planners are given the freedom to present inaccurate information. Plans represent a view of the future given a particular interpretation of information available at the time. Uncertainty can be quantified to represent probable outcomes, but it cannot be transformed into certainty. The desired outcome from a planning process is to give clarity to the enterprises' goals and possible options for realizing these goals. The path that leads to the goals must lead through a changing environment, and the path is subject to adjustments as the enterprise progresses.

Planning is often described in sequential steps. However, planning as learning means that the process is not linear and/or strictly sequential. Rather, the learning may cause enterprises to return to a previous step, making planning iterative in nature.

The context for each step is established by the previous learning. Starting with the strategic plan establishes the context by way of the Strategy Formulation process, which provided the insights necessary to create competitive advantage. In other words, the Planning Cycle resides within the context of Strategy Formulation.

Strategic Plan

At some point during the search for new insights in the Strategy Formulation process, it will be appropriate to put pen to paper and complete a Strategic Plan. This will be a long-term outlook of 5 to 15 years and will introduce financial outcomes, goals, and performance standards required to deliver the strategy. If done well, the strategic plan will:

- Frame the critical implementation actions
- Highlight the areas of leverage for financial success
- Point out potential weaknesses that must be overcome
- Highlight areas where the enterprise will need to develop or acquire capabilities

Some models of strategic planning emphasize Key Success Factors while others recommend Critical Objectives. Either method will outline ways to compete in the areas of:

- Size in the Market (market positioning required)
- Access to Resources/Customers
- Restrictions on Competitors' Options (patents, licensing requirements, etc.)
- Value Chain Positioning

The strategic plan should also include a cash flow forecast.

Although some strategic plans may imply *how* to carry out the strategy, most plans will contain mostly *what* needs to be done. The thrust of the plan should be what critical resources – people, money, technology, and time – are required and the outcome or value expected from this investment of resources. Major capital investment projects or programs are shown in the plan, along with their risk-adjusted Net Present Value and a summary of their critical components. The strategic plan starts the capital allocation process – choices regarding where to focus that scarce resource called money. The critical success measures that flow from this plan are integrated into the accountability system as the strategic control tool for the board or ownership committee – the ultimate approval body.

Business Plan

The Business Plan moves closer to the action, covering only 3 to 5 years, describing the *how*, and establishing more concrete financial numbers. Some call this the *programming* phase of the planning process (i.e., the business plan selects specific options and programs them for organizational action). Still, this is just a plan and not reality – remember that options change as the environment changes. Thus, the indicated performance targets within the business plan might be thought of as a range with plus or minus variances that increase as the time period moves farther out in years – year 4 is less accurate that year 2, for example.

The business plan will lay out critical objectives and financial projections over specific time periods, and it will also detail the human resources needs of the business – requirements for anticipated personnel training or re-development due to changing business demands. The business plan provides the context for the accountability system targets, giving meaning to the specific targets.

In an entrepreneurial world, the business plan is a necessary element for acquiring funding. Thus, for a small entrepreneurial business, the business plan may focus more heavily on how the business model works and the competencies of key personnel to deliver competitive advantage.

In a larger organization, the business plan is the second step (the first step is the strategic plan) in the capital resource allocation process. Here, the identification of options, along with costs of maintaining these options, might be a critical element of the plan.

For not-for-profit organizations, the business plan is a way to demonstrate that the organization's mission makes business sense as well as social sense. The business plan may highlight funding gaps and identify strategies for addressing funding risks. Or, the business plan should address where finite funds are best allocated to create the most 'benefit', however this may be measured.

In all cases, the business plan serves as a tool for identifying challenges and communicating the critical needs that must be addressed, so that the organization has time and understands the context for a response.

Operating Plan

The last step in the planning cycle, the Operating Plan, is the more detailed description of the first year of the business plan. This plan is often referred to as the Budget and thus mistakenly considered a finance activity, but as a connector of strategy to daily activities, the operating plan is the task-detailing part of planning and the finance role should only be that of consolidation. Operating plan preparation is a *line* function, presenting the tasks required for implementing the strategy-driven programs, the costs of doing these tasks, and expected outcomes.

The operating plan, usually achieved on a unit-by-unit or team-by-team basis, establishes personnel control numbers, capital budgets, and ongoing or operating business expenditures. The detail is specific enough to do bi-weekly cash flow planning and, if needed, to establish lines of credit with a bank or central cash management entity.

Usually laid out monthly, this Budget/Operating Plan is part of the operating control process for the enterprise. Approval of the operating plan by the board of trustees delegates expenditure authorization to the CEO and other managers in accord with the delegation of authority. "If it is not in, or implied by, the operating plan, it is not an approved expenditure and thus must be independently authorized" is the control motto of most CFOs.

The operating plan will present next year's performance targets for the accountability system.

Business Review Process

The key to creating a Business Management Cycle is the integration of these planning steps with the measurement and reporting of the accountability system – a business review process. This integration links the strategy to the operational aspects of the business and keeps a forward focus on all activities. This integration also assures that strategic thinking occurs on a continuing rather than a one-time basis and helps the organization learn to connect their operational decisions with strategy. Incorporating forward planning with the review process provides support for keeping the organization facing forward, even while doing a review process.

Once the Strategy Formulation has established how the enterprise is going to deliver its winning formula and an accountability system is operating, the cycle flows as shown in the accompanying diagram. Exact timing will vary, and unique events may dominate any one step in the cycle, but what is important is to keep the flow of planning activities connected to current performance.

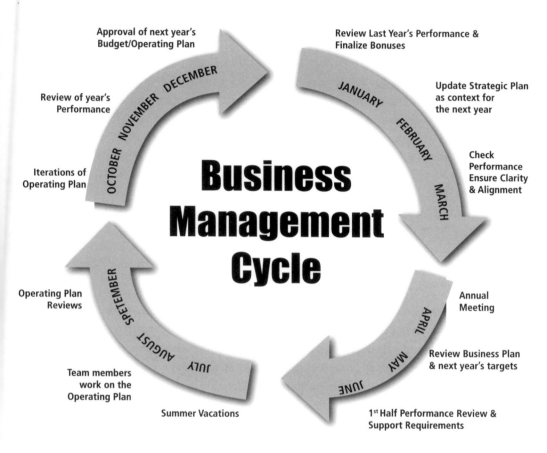

All meetings should be organized *From End to Start,* which means they should include both an overview of the expected outcomes from the meeting *and* some activity that links the expected conversations to the living performance vision and strategy. Participation should respect the *Contribution Defines Relationships* law. Be aware that the style of the meetings will create organizational stories that either reinforce the *perform-and-learn* culture or tell the organization that position power still reigns supreme. Exact timing of some review meetings might be determined by the timing of the financial closing for quarterly or monthly management accounts, although estimated information and timeliness are more useful than exact, but out-of-date, data.

First Quarter Business Period

Take a quick look back at the finalized (quality checked, if not audited) performance numbers from the previous year. Confirm compensation bonuses that hinged on the audited results of performance. Acknowledge efforts and successes of last year, and then move the conversation quickly to a forward focus.

Presenting updates to the strategic plan is a great way to ensure the conversation turns from the year-end review (looking backward) to a future focus, and you do not want to let the organization start the year facing backwards – especially if you had a very good or very bad year. That is, extraordinary outcomes are more prone to yield ongoing conversations about how they were achieved, which is looking backward. The strategy discussion provides great context for any *Direction* changes or adjustments and emphasizes the criticality of delivering the current targets in order to realize the desired outcome from the strategy. The relatively large competitor analysis portion of any strategy conversation connects well with emphasis on why the levels for the targets must be established as they are – *Competition Sets the Standards*.

In March, review performance for the first two months, but with a focus on ensuring that everyone has their performance connection well established. Ensuring clarity about performance expectations should happen early on in the year. It is very important that the year's required actions get underway early, and if you wait until late April to find out that areas of uncertainty exist, too much valuable time has been lost. Often, if critical actions have not occurred by the end of February, it is a sign that someone has lost focus or never had focus during the planning process.

Second Quarter Business Period

This quarter typically contains the Annual Meeting in April or May, which is often an event for acknowledging accomplishments as part of a review of the previous year. This is fine, of course, and even necessary, but you still want to use this opportunity to work on the alignment of future objectives with these stakeholders. Use the same concept as with performance reviews: start with the backward look but find a connection to the future whenever possible – summarize the past by saying what it means for the future.

While an Annual Meeting might more heavily involve external stakeholders, internal business continues, and the second quarter is the time to present the updated 3 or 5-Year Business Plan. Last quarter's review of strategic realignment gave the context for the business plan. The year is now nearly half over and progress toward the year-end targets takes on more urgency. If something is missing and leadership support is required, this may be the last chance to make necessary adjustments in order to meet year-end targets.

Integrating short-term planning is consistent with this urgent conversation. Decisions about required actions to achieve the year-end targets will benefit from the context provided by the next three-year outlook. The business plan is also the place for teams to ballpark the target levels for the following year. Before they work out the details of the operating plan, it is important for them to get a feel for the acceptability of these target levels, and the business plan lets teams demonstrate the competitiveness of their target proposals.

Third Quarter Business Period

This is Operating Plan/Budget preparation time, even though this is often the summer holiday period, with July and August requiring scheduling adjustments for most meetings so that key players will be available. You can lighten the meeting load and let staff work on the details of the operating plan for presentation in September.

The business plan, and not last year's operating plan, must be the context for doing next year's operating plan. However, you might notice that when this work gets separated from the planning process and is finance-driven as a separate activity set, there is often the temptation to use last year's operating plan as the starting point for this *budget* activity. This is like backing into the next year – the context becomes historic and not strategic. So, you will want to present the first draft of the operating plan based upon the context set by the business plan discussion last quarter.

Operating Plan/Budget review and finalization will take several weeks, if not a couple of months, of iteration before it is ready for board approval during the 12th month. Use this meeting to declare performance targets for the upcoming year. These targets will also be the subject of an iteration process that should start early. If the teams' plans do not make good business sense, now is the time to change them or to consider the need to change team members.

Fourth Quarter Business Period

The end of the year is in sight. It will now be apparent that the performance targets will either be met or missed, and meetings during this period are used to review what the final outcomes will look like and to finalize plans and targets for the next year. Projects or expenditure actions required to make the next year a success can be presented for approval at this time.

The status of performance delivery will play a key role in determining the amount of Space available to the team(s) *next* year. Consistent delivery of performance relative to targets establishes a track record of responsibility, and more *Space* in the coming year is possible. On the other hand, failure to establish a positive track record may require the reduction of *Space* and/or other actions to assure that individuals or teams are capable of handling the responsibilities associated with their performance commitments.

The Enterprise's Performance Conversation

You might consider this integration of planning, reviewing, authorizing, and communicating as the *Enterprise's Performance Conversation*, which begins with Direction and ends with accomplishment. All basic business controls should be connected to this Business Management Cycle. Use these meetings for authorization of activities that require higher-level approvals than can be granted in the operating plan approval, or you can allow the meetings to trigger smaller, follow-up meetings to discuss a particular project or issue – but connect every one of your internal processes to this Business Management Cycle.

This integration is very important, or the organization will separate performance from processes and procedures. We have seen situations where expenditure authorizations and/or procurement procedures were allowed to operate outside of these performance-based business meetings. This practice allowed *position power* to override *performance power* and maintained bureaucratic procedures that were seemingly unconnected to the performance demands of the business. If a performance connection is to be maintained, then every activity of the enterprise must be *in the service* of performance and cannot operate outside of the organization's performance conversation.

Chapter 14

Success is the old ABC – Ability, Breaks and Courage.
Charles Luckman

The Last Bits

As we near the end of this transformational journey, the ingredients for a relational organization are now clear:

- **Relational Leadership** acknowledges individual uniqueness, addresses relational needs, and keeps the individual responsible for maintaining connection with the enterprise's performance vision as competitive forces change the goals.

- **A Living Vision and Strategy** provides the performance vision and identifies Strategic Intent for organizational focus.

- **A Business-Purpose Defined Team Structure** establishes an entrepreneurial, market-driven internal environment for the enterprise.

- **A Strategy-Linked and Cascaded Accountability System** supplies tangible goals and creates the assurance framework to allow the elimination of command-and-control style procedures.

Even the process for mixing and baking the ingredients, the Business Management Cycle, has been set out, and now it is time to summarize some of the critical ideas to determine if anything important might be missing from this relational management recipe.

Observe Your Being

One of the best ways to stay connected with the relational leadership model is to check on yourself from time to time. Here are a few leadership perspectives that might become apparent in this act of inward looking. We will speak of these perspectives as ways of being that can impede leading under the *perform-and-learn* model. These ways of being are not necessarily wrong and may be appropriate in specific situations, but our point here is that you must be able to observe your *way of being* in all situations and to see their use as a choice. Then you can be responsible for the consequences that may result, and you will be able to adjust your way of being as required.

- **Being in Judgment** – Under the command-and-control model, the act of judgment is almost synonymous with leadership. You might be asking, "After all, isn't that the job of leadership, to pass judgment and make decisions?" This is true, of course, but we tend to move from judging risk to "being in judgment" of people without making any distinction. When judgment of others is present, the relationship changes. When judgment is present, Support and Coaching is not an available relationship option and responsibility for the performance outcomes is transferred back to the leader.

- **Being in Blame** – This is a backward-facing position that takes the focus away from the performance vision. Judgment and condemnation are often elements of this conversation. Regular use of this way of being will result in an organization more concerned about looking good than doing well. People will usually have a story about how the situation was/is beyond their control.

- **Being in Role** – This is a situation wherein identity gets commingled with the position or role and you can lose not only your special contribution but that of others as well. The need to be seen as in charge and to have the answer excludes the contribution of others. When one's role is taking precedence over Me Inc., it signals the organization that command-and-control is back is session.

- **Being in Knowing** – When knowing or being right surfaces, interactions move back to an exchange of opinions. Collaboration is difficult, if not impossible, and the ability to create is severely restricted. Would you rather be right or successful in realizing your objective?

- **Being the Parent** – The Parent/Child relational model combines several of the above ways of being together. We often move into this way of being without realizing either the model or its impact. Telling becomes the mode of communication – we can almost hear ourselves saying, "Here, do it this way," or "Do it because I said to!" Staff members then move into either a compliant/dependency relationship or the rebellious teenager role, and we are back to a command-and-control response.

Support and Coach

Always, always provide *Direction* and work to ensure that there is clarity regarding the Performance Vision of the Enterprise (i.e., can the other party tell you what is expected?). Then manage the *Space* by using tools appropriate to each situation – Clarity, Context, Challenge, Counsel, Collaboration, Demonstration, and Celebration – to provide what might be missing for them.

Listen first to appreciate the other party's context when working with them. In the beginning of the transformation to the relational model, staff is likely to define your words and actions using a leader-as-parent context. In this dependent world, requests are taken as orders rather than as guidance toward the goal, and the leader can be blamed if anything goes wrong: "I did what I was told – you can't blame me." You can avoid this dynamic by verifying what has been heard after conversations. Acknowledge the other's context before moving to your agenda – it will give them space to appreciate your context and open the way for a responsible conversation.

Even with the best of efforts, you will still be required to deal with performance failure. Just remember, performance failure is not failure of the individual as a possibility, but rather, a failure to meet their accountabilities. Don't condemn the person – they are still a possibility. Hold them accountable and work with them to discover the failure mode. Failure is obviously *not* their desired outcome – they did not plan to screw up. There are three fundamental reasons why people fail, and each failure mode can be described in terms of what is missing for *them*:

1. **Missing the Possibility** – The person does not see the desired outcome as representing a possibility for them. They lack belief in the possibility or simply see the outcome as just so far beyond their skill and knowledge level that it is impossible. For such an individual, "trying" will be the definition of success. Begin a coaching conversation about possibilities.

2. **Missing the Skills** – The person does not possess the skills or knowledge required to realize their defined possibility. They think they can achieve this possibility, but in reality, they need skill development to be able to reach their goals. They may even say they are doing one thing while you observe them doing something entirely different. Skills can be developed through training and practice, and if you have the luxury of time and money, this failure mode can be overcome.

3. **Missing the Problem** – This mode is popularly manifested as "solving the wrong problem." The person's concept of how to reach the goal is somehow flawed – problem definition is incomplete. This is a need to go back to square one and rethink the problem in order to fill in the gaps in this individual's comprehension of the problem.

Missing the Possibility

Start your coaching conversation by looking first for possibility misalignment. Ask the person to describe the expected outcome, and then ask how that outcome is critical for them (i.e., if they deliver the outcome, what might it do for them?). This will tell you if they think the outcome is a possibility and represents something that is important to them. If they do see the outcome as possible, with something in it for them, look for missing skills.

However, if they describe the outcome but there is no real energy in the description, the possibility is missing for them. They know what is required but are disconnected from it as a personal possibility. Begin a conversation that explores the alignment of their personal purpose (passion) in life with the objectives.

If they continue to fail to see the outcome as a possibility, give them a choice to accept the challenge or decline to participate. Do not lower the standard, which is not within your control anyway – *Competition Sets the*

Standard. If alignment is not possible, get a different person to do that job. You are in essence giving up on them by defining them as a possibility to work elsewhere, as this person will never be successful at the level competition demands unless they see possibility in the outcome and can find a link with their personal purpose in life and the enterprise's vision.

When the person does not want the possibility, they will never deliver the required standard of performance. You cannot take people where they do not want to go. You cannot make a person into a possibility they do not want to become. No matter how strongly you define that person as a possibility for that performance, they will not get there. When it is clear that the possibilities you see for the individual and your performance vision do not match the possibilities they can see for themselves, it is time to quit putting forth the effort. If you care for them at all, help them move out of that position and/or out of the enterprise.

Missing the Skills

If you have confirmed that possibility alignment is present, you can now move on to an examination of skill deficiencies. Begin this conversation by assuming that they have the skills and accept that they are accurately describing their actions (i.e., can they see their performance realistically?).

- Ask them what actions they have taken in pursuit of their goal.

- Ask them what they expected to result from these actions.

- Ask them what the results were.

- Ask for and listen to their story.

Replay to them what they have told you – use their words as much as possible to confirm that you heard them accurately. Listen from their perspective until you understand how they view their skills.

If possible, watch them in action. Again without judgment, describe to them what you see. If that picture matches the picture they described to you, then it is probable that they are realistic about their skills and know how and when to apply them. If not, their "theory espoused" is different from their "theory in action," and you have a learning opportunity to teach them the skills needed to put their espoused theory into action.

If you have the ability and knowledge, coach them on the skills and their application. If you do not have the knowledge or the time to coach the individual, hire a specialist. Hold them accountable to learn the skills from the specialist – use performance measures to follow up.

Determining if the proper skills are present is a critical step and perhaps the most difficult in this process. It is far easier to justify your judgment that skills are not the issue by rationalizing your belief in them, by seeing them as a possibility – even while they are floundering in failure. When someone is "in over their head," telling them you believe in them is of little value – it may even be cruel! They are so lost that they do not know what to do or how to do it, and they cannot even find the words to express the problem. When you continue to encourage them to achieve something patently beyond their ability, they will fail and (rightly) blame you as a leader for allowing them to fail.

Perhaps the best example of this leadership conduct is in professional baseball, when young players are promoted to the big leagues before they are ready. When they fail, their confidence is so damaged that they seldom recover and either stay in the minor leagues for the rest of their playing career or leave the sport entirely. The same thing can happen to a young professional in the business world if a leader does not take the time to properly assess if they lack some skills.

It is necessary to always keep an eye on the missing skills issue, even as you move to a *missing-the-problem* analysis. If performance difficulties continue, and as the problem identification brings clarity, you can be fairly certain of a skill problem. Watch for this to occur as you progress.

Missing the Problem

If alignment of individual purpose with the goals of the enterprise is evident and you are fairly certain that skills are present, then problem definition is at the heart of the failure. Your employee is working on a different problem than the one that will yield the desired results. Our experience indicates that this is the most common issue – people define the problem incorrectly. It is also the easiest issue to correct.

Defining the problem incorrectly can often be identified by statements about "they" as the problem. For example: "They will not let me do that." Or: "They will not do what I need or want." This is a situation for inquiry learning (discussed in *Chapter 5*) and requires an in-depth examination designed to uncover hidden assumptions and beliefs (their truths) about the problem and its solution. These beliefs are blocking access to the real problem and potential solutions.

For example, we were working with a manager who needed to dramatically reduce his budget. A key line item was a "commitment" to a government agency associated with a planned work program. This commitment had been made several years earlier under different industry conditions. To meet current budget constraints, the manager had to eliminate this expenditure commitment.

The inquiry conversation started by asking the manager to define the problem. The manager said, "The problem is, they won't let me change the work program."

"Why won't they let you change the work program?" he was asked.

"Because this is a commitment," he said.

"Why is it a commitment?" he was asked.

"Because I said I would do it when we started working with them," he said.

"Why is that a problem?"

"Because I gave them my word."

"So, the problem is that you gave them your word?"

"Well, when you say it that way, yes the problem is my word," he said. "I really do not know if they will change the program, as I do not want to go back on my word by asking."

The problem this manager was dealing with was not, "They won't let me change the program." The problem was the manager's relationship to his word. Asking to change the program because of different industry conditions felt like a loss of his integrity. He was avoiding the real problem and trying to get the government to change the program without him confronting the fact that he was the one who made the original commitment. Once he could see the problem as himself, he was able to hold a straightforward conversation with the government representatives and alter the commitment to fit current industry conditions.

As you look at the previous example, you might relate to this as a common situation wherein the beginning conversation is around "they" as the problem. Actually, the problem is often the opposite of "they." "We" are the problem – our relationship to the dilemma is what gets in the way of the solution.

Each conversation to uncover hidden assumptions will be specific; therefore, the solution will be specific. The leader must find the problem by holding a two-way conversation and not by making a "do this, not that" directive.

An often useful approach is to flip the situation. Take an exact opposite view of the circumstances – assume the opposite is true. If the problem is being defined as "They won't let me change it." Try asking, "What if they did want you to change it? What then would be the problem?" This often gets immediately to the problem at hand. In the above case, the problem would then be "I would have to change a commitment I made." The real problem is not them, but rather, it is us – a different problem that requires a different solution.

Show Me the Money

A management model would not be complete without a view of compensation. As a management methodology, the relational model may not be about the money, but get compensation wrong and your conversations and concerns *will* be about the money! And getting it wrong is very easy to do. Remember, the compensation strategy must take the three relational laws into account and cannot exist independent of Vision and Strategy.

If what gets measured gets attention, what gets rewarded tells the organization what leadership *really* values. If these two factors are out of alignment, it causes major problems. The compensation strategy in a performance-connected organization should do the following:

- Support the Accountability System by reinforcing the focus on the links to the business strategy

- Reinforce the Competition Sets the Standard law by allowing employees to earn a competitive wage

- Provide opportunity for superior business performance to deliver superior compensation reward

- Reinforce the team concept while acknowledging individual contribution.

First, give up the concept that your reward system must be fair, which is an ideal rather than a reality anyway. Compensation is not a fair process. This is not to say it should be unfair, but rather, it is just not possible to deliver a completely fair compensation system because fairness is a relative concept whose definition resides in the mind of each individual. What is fair to you is not necessarily fair to another person. Any system that is promoted by leadership as being fair will fail to meet that standard for far more than half its recipients. The relational model will suffer as the people who promote the system as fair will be thought of as being untruthful. Who wants a relationship with untruthful people?

Basic salary is not a motivational factor. It is a hygiene factor, necessary but not sufficient in and of itself to motivate your staff. If it is too low, however, the level of base pay can de-motivate staff, and annual pay increases or salary adjustments have a motivational half-life of less than one week. In fact, when annual salary adjustments are linked to some form of performance using a standardized grading system (forced ranking), they are de-motivating for at least 70 % of those receiving the adjustment. Think of it this way: if a system uses a 1 to 5 (5 being the best or highest) scale that allows 5-10% to get 5's, 10-20 % to get 4's, and the rest of staff 3's or lower, some 70 to 85% of staff are being told they are average or below. Few people are flattered by being told they are average – are you? Add to this the impact of near decision-time events that largely determine most leader's rating assessments, and de-motivation and cries of unfairness increase geometrically. Why would anyone wish to operate a system in which they pay money to de-motivate the majority of their staff?

In order to meet all of what a compensation strategy should do to support performance, it is necessary to segregate the compensation strategy into individual elements or components. These elements are:

- Base Pay – an individual element that can be matched to the market for comparable skills, knowledge, and contribution. Attention all readers familiar with the most popular systems used to establish salary grades and ranges for positions based upon size of the organization or level of responsibility: do not use them. We did not mention anything about position, measures for size, impact, or etc. in our discussion in this book – for we are after contribution. Professional Ladders are the closest thing to a systematic process for grading on the basis of skills, knowledge, and contribution. Base Pay should be thought of as the purchasing of Me Inc.'s skills and knowledge – not buying the person's time.

- Gain Sharing – a team-based element that relates delivery of outstanding competitive business performance to above-market compensations. Integrated with the accountability system, this element supports team commitment and aligns the organization with the business strategy.

- Recognition Compensation – a bonus process for acknowledgement of individuals or small groups through immediate recognition. Again, attention readers familiar with currently popular systems of richly rewarding senior executives, who seem to get "money for nothing and chicks for free" to quote from a Dire Straits song: forget them. We did not say this is an annual or even monetary bonus, but instead stressed an immediate recognition element. It can be money, but there are lots of other things this bonus could also be.

The details for this strategy should be business- and industry-specific – Competition Sets the Standards. The key is to have all three elements. Overtly link contribution and competition, tie the system to the *Direction* piece of the leadership model, support teams first and individuals second, and base the entire compensation strategy on the enterprise's competitive performance.

You will want to keep the framework straightforward to help staff understand, and the bottom line for them needs to be that employees get paid at market rates thereby reinforcing competitive understanding. If employees can earn above-market wages for delivery of superior business results, staff can see that what is expected of them is valued. By not putting every bit of compensation into base salary, the fixed burden of the wage structure is reduced, and the framework is flexible so that you can use it to cover a broad spectrum of situations.

The system is far easier to design than it is to administer, and that is why most human resource functions often will reject it as a possibility. Finding the comparable market for a set of skills is a difficult and continuing exercise, but the results are worth the effort. No one gets it right (again, compensation is not fair), but it will keep the organization engaged in the right conversation and it will stop the organization from paying money to de-motivate people.

We suggest that implementation of this compensation strategy follow the implementation of the accountability system. There is often pressure to change the compensation practices first – usually with an incentive scheme – as nearly everyone thinks it will motivate the organization. In reality, these rush-to-judgment incentive schemes often provide rewards for picking the low hanging fruit as they send the message that "it is about the money" rather than about performance. It will serve you to remember that you cannot buy the heart; even the best incentive schemes are only renting it.

The End Perspective

This brings us to the end of the transformation process for moving the organization from its foundation of command-and-control to the *Perform and Learn* culture that engages the whole person in a performance commitment. The end of the transformation process does not mean that leaders get to sit back and rest, however. The relational model puts people in relationship with the enterprise's performance vision; and like all relationships, this relationship must be tended.

The Business Management Cycle is a useful tool for this relationship tending process, but because this work is about engaging people as human beings rather than as objects, leaders cannot run this system like it is a project management process (i.e., today the schedule calls for a strategy review, and we will wait until next week to complete the performance report, etc.). The performance vision is always responding to environmental change, people's lives are always responding to personal change, and the two will drift apart without guidance. The living performance vision defines the context for each activity within the Business Management Cycle, but these activities must also blend with the condition of Me Inc. As change transforms all parties' perspectives, the following question must be asked continually: "What does the relationship now need for the connection to be maintained?"

Leaders are in the business of matchmaking – finding the match between Me Inc. and Business Inc. Once the match is made, they must tend the relationship, coaching Me Inc. to contribute to helping Business Inc. follow its strategy, even while that strategy migrates. Leadership is not a job for the lazy. It is not a job for the egotist. It is a job for those who believe in the power of the human heart to create.

The industrial revolution taught leaders how to put the *hands* to work. Business schools have taught leaders how to put the *head* to work. Now it is time to put the *heart* to work in conjunction with the *hands* and *head*. The living vision gives space for the *heart*, the strategy gives focus to the *head*, and the accountability system keeps the *hands* in motion. The person is in balance with the enterprise, and the needs of Me Inc. and the needs of Business Inc. are aligned.

We are convinced that the *perform-and-learn* context is required to take organizational performance to the next level, but unlearning years of *command-and-control* indoctrination means reinvention of one's self on a daily basis – *from end to start*, each day. Relational management is both a simple and a complex concept. It is not rocket science, but much simpler and much harder at once – it is relational. May all your relationships be built on common purpose. May all your relationships give you the freedom to be you. May you always be accountable for who you are.

Getting Into Action

The discussion in this book has been along the lines of a classic paradigm shift – head and heart stuff. Although we have provided a guide for practices that transition leadership from the parental, or hero-as-leader, model to a relational model, the real how-to-do-it portion (or hands stuff) has largely been left until now. We are going to use the appendix to take you through the key implementation steps for introducing this Relational Management Model. Our assumption is that the concepts are now quite well understood, and thus, this overview will be brief but practical.

Aligning at the Top

Before any transformation within the organization can start, the entire leadership team must be aligned with organizational direction and the Relational Management Model.

It is essential that the entire leadership team take the time to define new possibilities for themselves and the enterprise. New actions and new behaviors will not happen until new possibilities are established. We have seen numerous attempts to bypass this first step, and we usually hear the same story: "We are all together on this one – let's get going." In truth, however, "we" are *never* all on the same page. Aside from a superficial understanding of the change process in which they are involved, each member of the leadership team has a different view (and definition) of what the work is about, where the enterprise is headed, or what their role is in the change at hand. They speak differently about the reason and the desired result of these changes, and they act differently in delivering the process to achieve these changes. They pull the organization in different directions as a result.

> *For staff, misalignment is very easy to spot. We remember a great management team session where a major business change was about to occur. Three groups in the business were being combined, and the management teams from each group were invited to an away day by the three group leaders. The purpose was to present a unified front and to get the team moving toward integration of the work.*
>
> *The first group leader stood up to speak: "We are all agreed on what is to happen. There are a large number of concerns, and we will have to be very cautious how we proceed with the details."*
>
> *The second one stood up: "We are all agreed on what is to happen. This is an exciting time, and we need to look at what is possible here. We need to generate the options for moving forward and create some exciting possibilities."*
>
> *The third one stood up: "We all agreed on what has to happen. It is clear what needs doing and we need to get on and do it. The train is leaving the station and you all better be on it!"*
>
> *The nervous laughter was audible amongst the assembled management teams and the challenge was immediate. This "we-are-united" act lasted less than 30 minutes into the meeting.*

A common leadership language is a very important part of being all together, but merely agreeing to show a united front does not work. Leadership language is the first means (the second is your deeds) by which the leadership conveys their understanding to an organization. It is important to use the same words to describe the same things. Often we have heard the same words used to describe different things or different words to describe the same things, and when this happens, stories of confusion at the top are created and this perceived lack of cohesion and alignment is used to undermine the change by those seeking to derail the process.

What to do

First achieve clarity about the *End* in the form of answers to these basic questions:

1. "Why are we undertaking this transformation? Or "What is the Purpose of this transformation?" And "Why are we undertaking this now?"

2. "What do we expect to accomplish?" Or "What will success look like in, say, three years?"

3. "What will be different about the way the organization functions to achieve these goals?"

4. "What will be different about how the Leadership Team works, individually and collectively, to support this change?"

When answering the first set of questions, it is easy to make the past strategy appear to have been all wrong, as in something is broken and needs to be fixed, or perhaps to say, "We did the wrong things to get here." In all likelihood, that approach will make many people within the enterprise feel that all their previous years were failures and their efforts a waste of time. A common reaction to being made wrong is anger and subsequent rejection of what is being proposed.

Whether things in the past were as good as they could have been is immaterial. What is material is how dearly the people most closely identified with past initiatives will hold onto them. The more you make them appear to have been wrong, the more they will resent and obstruct the changes you are trying to initiate.

So, be generous to the past, both in terms of accomplishments and methods of proceeding, and avoid this pitfall, but remember that it is important to honor the past while facing the future and seeing its possibilities. The message is that the enterprise has had many years of success, and the introduction of the relational model and these leadership practices is being undertaken in order to take the enterprise into the future. Your response to stakeholders who ask "Why the change?" will be "What might this model make possible that the old model could not deliver?"

One method used by a successful team was to create a "compelling reason for change." A senior executive called his team together, took out a pen and drew a simple x and y axis. He drew one line rising from the bottom left to the top right and another falling from the top left to the bottom right. The first line he labeled cost, and the second line he labeled return on capital invested. Pointing at the intersection of the two lines he said, "We are here!"

He made no comment on how they got there – he just gave them the bare facts. He added, "If we do nothing, this organization will decrease in numbers, will not be able to justify further capital investment, and we will be gone. Our community will be economically poorer for our children. If we take action, now, we will protect our own jobs, improve our prosperity, and keep our industry going for at least another 25 years."

That organization delivered $1 billion of free cash flow from that location for that year and for each of the next 5 years.

Simple, yes, but powerful and engaging – from end to start.

When answering questions 2 through 4 as posed on page 201 (What do we expect .... and what will be different ....?), the leadership team must develop a common understanding of what is expected from the transformation – *Their Performance Vision*. Expected outcomes should encompass activities in two distinct areas:

1. The first outcomes to be defined are those in the area of performance. What are the tangible aspects of performance that will be measured and improved as a result of the transformation? What are the targets and timeframes for each measurement area? We call these *"future performance criteria."*

2. The second outcome area to be defined is behavioral. The leadership team must define the behaviors and actions they expect to see in employees and themselves as a result of using the *perform-and-learn* model. We are not talking about a list of values, although these may be a part of the behavior equation. As you have seen, these are relational interactions. We call these *"future behaviors."*

Keep these initial performance measurement criteria simple and limited in number. The objective is to tap the power of non-complex, challenging, mobilizing, and enabling goals to which the members of the organization can first connect and then figure out their own way to these endpoint goals.

How to do it

The process for clarifying Leadership's vision uses the *Involve Others in the Conversation* practice, inviting the broader team into this conversation about the future. Leadership workshops work well to accomplish this task by laying the foundation for common understandings and definitions. The leader must sponsor this work, clearly identifying the outcomes desired from each workshop. However, he/she may well ask others to prepare and facilitate each working session. In fact, we recommend that a leader regularly use a third party facilitator so that the leader can be a fulltime contributor to the meeting content while someone else manages the meeting process.

Future Performance Criteria

Take the leadership team away from their daily routine, and in collaboration with them, create a future picture of the organization. Work with selected background materials, use the experience and instincts of the team members, and bring in someone to provide challenge and to avoid group-think. Keep it simple. Choose some future time – about 2 to 5 years from now. Keep the timeframe beyond tomorrow but within mental reach.

Working in small groups (from 2 to 7 depending on the size of the leadership team), ask the participants to describe:

- Things they believe the organization must be doing better 3 years from now.

- Things they must be doing in a different form than at present.

- Things they should not be doing at all.

Bring the participants back together and discuss or debate, to a point of general consensus, the key areas of performance that could be different in the future. Then ask the team to set measurable targets in each area for various points in time. Define and record these targets – these should be big-picture goals for the entire organization. Establish a simple, paper system for measuring and reporting progress on these performance targets. Later, when you develop your accountability system, incorporate these targets into that system.

It is likely that the first piece of resistance behavior will surface when target setting begins. There may be several strong voices in the room expressing a need for the system to come first, or for a study to be done, or for more data to be gathered. This is avoidance behavior and probably driven by worst fears about the change because the new possibilities for the individuals on the leadership team are not yet established.

Handle avoidance behavior by first acknowledging it. Ask, "What might happen if the system is not set up right now?" Ask, "How will this be a problem?" Acknowledge any potential issues, but do outline for them what *is* a real issue and what *is not* a real issue. Establish the possibility of returning to this point in the future and ask them to consider the possibility that you might not need to set up such a formal system first. Perhaps ask those who are concerned to take responsibility for setting up this formal system for future use, but be clear that you will review this system at some specific future time. You need to buy time here – not foster resistance that will ultimately hold you back. Gently *call* or expose this behavior by acknowledging that feelings of concern exist – then move forward.

If the changes in performance expectations identified are not substantial, challenge the need for a transformation. If leadership believes that small performance improvements are sufficient, the pull of a new future will not be adequate to engage the organization – it will not present any new possibilities for them. The paradigm change to this relational methodology is not required. Work with existing process until the business need for change is stronger.

Future Behaviors

With the establishment of measurable big-picture performance expectations, the discussion can move to the relational perspective, behavioral expectations. You can use the same process, but with a personal twist at the end. Look at different areas of the business and build a picture of how people will be interacting when the relational model is implemented – think *Contribution Defines Relationships*. Choose areas where interfaces are important. As examples, consider some of the following:

- Interactions within the leadership team
- Leadership team's interactions with the entire organization
- Engineering and operations interfaces

- Sales and operations interactions
- Programs and finance relationships

The leadership team should picture how these key areas of interface might interact (i.e., in story form, you might describe how they may be working). Choose a future point in time and ask individuals to describe how, under this relational approach, work will be getting done between these areas of interface. Let them tell the story and ask others to collaborate with them. See if people have common views of this new model.

After the small group discussions, enter into a plenary group dialogue so that the team begins to develop common definitions and understandings of what they expect. Keep a record of the outcomes so that the leadership team can revisit them as the transformation progresses.

If this sounds like a lot of conversations and meetings, you are correct. Building a background of understanding within the leadership team is foundational to success and will pay back the time spent ten-fold. Do not skip this foundation building. Be prepared to do a return run after the first year to reconnect the leadership and go deeper into what is required next.

Personal Commitments

After the group has reached its general understanding about desired behaviors, move the focus to individual/personal behaviors. Ask each participant to spend some individual quiet time, thinking about what this change will mean for them personally.

- What does this transformation in the leadership paradigm mean for them?
- What might they lose?
- What might they gain?
- What will they need to do differently?
- What will they need to stop doing?
- What will they need to start doing?

Ask each member of the leadership team to write down the answers to these questions, and after they have spent at least one night reflecting on the personal impact, have each of them write a personal performance commitment statement regarding their role in this transformation process. Within this commitment statement, have them include their own personal possibility: "What is in this for them?" Ask them to define what they will personally be accountable for in the transformation process. Record these for that second leadership discussion about one year into this relational transformation process.

The foundation is nearly set. The leadership team:

- Has defined the business outcomes from which to measure the transformation process

- Understands their personal stake in this matter

- Has linked their personal purpose to the business purpose, and

- Has identified their accountabilities

Start a performance conversation with each individual to develop the linkage between their passion, contribution, and accountability. Spend a few minutes acknowledging the individual contributions expected from each, or do this publicly with at least a selected few individuals. Over the next few months, take the time to acknowledge the expected contribution from each person, and the foundation will be well established for beginning the transformation. Through this performance conversation, you will close the loop within the leadership team. They will be performance connected – *Purpose*, *Identity*, and *Accountability*.

After completing the alignment and connection process with the leadership team, it is possible that team members might begin to lead from their personal connection to the performance vision. More likely though, after their return to the old daily routine and its culture of leader-as-hero expectations, old behaviors will re-surface. Even though members of the leadership team may talk about the new behaviors and bold goals, their practices could well reflect old habits.

This return to old habits happens because each member of the leadership team has not developed new possibilities for the individuals with whom they work – they haven't yet redefined them as possibilities for performance. Their interactions with these individuals will reflect the old possibilities – possibilities to be right, etc. In addition, existing organizational processes will continue to be administered within the command-and-control paradigm, pulling the leadership back into old practices.

The new behaviors will require reinforcement, and each member of the leadership team will be required to look at (i.e., reflect upon) the possibilities they hold for their staff. This is an ideal opportunity for coaching, and either team members can coach one another or you can utilize outside executive coaching. The choice depends upon the needs and coaching skills within the team, but our experience-based recommendation is to invest in good quality executive coaching to avoid any loss of momentum due to backsliding leadership behavior.

At the very least, there will be the need for an environment in which members of the leadership team can challenge each other. As leadership makes a transformation to the relational leadership model, it is critical for them to have some reflective process for understanding how they appear to others. This reflection should be part of the identity formation process centered on understanding strengths and how to leverage them for better performance. Some training may be involved, but good coaching is the art of reflecting to achieve clarity with regard to choices, consequences, and options. Good coaching will be able to help the person bring their authentic self and the relational leadership model together.

With the leadership team engaged, we will now look at how to expand upon this beginning, including the full organization in a manner that engages them rather than evoking major cynicism.

Starting the Organizational Connection

When leadership introduces these new challenges to the organization, they will be heard by staff within the existing hierarchical, command-and-control context. Until new stories are created, staff will define words and actions from their historical context. Thus, the next step is to introduce the organization to this Relational Management Model – to help them understand the distinction of *perform-and-learn*.

We do not recommend that you introduce the organization to the relational model by undertaking a massive cultural change initiative. We do suggest that you start by looking first at what is missing for the organization currently. You can then let the organization learn by examining a single project (or a couple of projects) and learn-by-doing as the relational model is integrated into the structure and accountability processes. Not only does it generally make sense to introduce new ideas in areas where they will provide the most leverage, but focusing the application allows leaders to practice relational leadership and to observe the benefits in a relatively contained environment.

Start with the Missing

Depending on the size and status of the organization, looking for what is missing may be as simple as doing an inquiry session with a few of the opinion leaders from the staff. Working with this focus group, you may be able to see how current processes limit or restrict people from connecting with the needs of the business. Alternatively, you might ask someone outside the organization to observe several meetings and then describe (not judge) what they observed – play back a story of how people interacted. Meetings are generally a cameo of the larger organization and allow an experienced observer to detect unwritten rules of the organization, or cultural norms that may contradict the strategy.

Perhaps you already know what might be missing, perhaps strategic clarity or an organizational misperception of competitive performance, or you may have data that indicates issues – perhaps customer retention is competitively low or staff turnover is competitively high. These symptoms can guide you to the area of the business that will benefit most from the introduction of this relational model.

What happens next

Whatever area you choose, get agreement within the leadership team on the initial project – enroll every member of the leadership team in a commitment to supporting this project and be clear about their specific accountabilities for its success.

Staff the project team as a business-purpose team. Choose team members with complementary contributions in order to provide a well-rounded perspective. Select individuals by considering contributions of technical knowledge, business knowledge, people skills, communication skills, etc. Keep the team size to fewer than 10, and preferably in the 6-8 person range.

Implement this starting project using the Leadership Model: Direction, Boundaries, then Support requirements. Set the *Direction* with the Project Team. Engage them in a discussion linking the expected outcomes to the vision of the organization – *From End to Start*. This will give them the big-picture context for their work. Use the following process steps to increase engagement:

- *Be open and honest.* If you have made specific decisions about the project, be clear about what has been decided, and where input is still possible, designate whether it will be input from the team or from others. If you are uncertain, let the team know that also. The quickest and easiest way to establish credibility is to be honest and say what is on your mind, even if you think this is not what others want to hear.

- *Link their Purpose.* Have the team write a "Project Purpose Statement." Ask the team to describe how this work fits with the direction for the larger enterprise. The team should have enough information to undertake this as their first task – draft a project purpose statement. One approach is to do a problem definition – what is the problem this project solves. During this process, the team members will begin to make their own personal links to the purpose of the project. When reviewing this work, hold with this discussion until you are certain that everyone is on the same page.

- *Set Boundaries.* What defines the Space available to the team? By now you know: use self-teaching to engage. Ask the team about their understanding of the boundaries. What can they do and not do? We suggest that you set the initial boundaries a bit wider than normal and give this team the opportunity to surprise you with their creativity. If this strategy makes you uncomfortable, increase the regularity of communications feedback from the team so that you are well informed of their thinking as they progress.

- *Establish Accountability.* Define the metrics that are important for success. Ask the team to identify performance targets for these metrics. Agree on specific targets, milestones, and timeframes for delivery.

- *Define support processes.* Once *Direction* (i.e., purpose and accountability) and *Boundaries* are defined, establish the process for providing resources and support. What resources will the team require? How will they communicate progress and resolve obstacles? Ah, you have noticed – these are questions for them to answer for you rather than something for you to tell them.

The Project Process

Since a Project Team is an enterprise in its own right, we will follow this first project through its initial implementation steps. This will allow us to demonstrate how our relational model elements are integrated to build a performance-driven organization. The focus is initially on the team leader, who is the CEO of this project team enterprise.

Set the Direction

The writing of the project team's purpose statement should solidify the *Direction* element of the Leadership Model for them. This is like an organization doing Mission, Vision, and Strategy work, but within a much narrower frame. An external coach may help this team, both facilitating the process and teaching the inquiry method of learning.

> *If we can break the discussion for a brief minute, it may be important to distinguish between the use of a coach or coach/facilitator and an external consultant. We use the term coach because we believe it important that the individual is actively engaged in teaching the people these relational methodologies. It has been our experience that consultants are used to bring in expertise but not required to leave this expertise embedded when they leave. A coach is engaged to do just that, to bring in expertise and leave it embedded. This expertise will be of continuing value as you broaden the implementation and as other changes require further learning down the road.*

Taking into account the outcomes discussed with the larger business unit leadership team, the project team must build a common understanding of what they have been asked to do. At this point, each individual will have heard the discussion with the leadership team from the vantage of their individual context and history. They must now develop common definitions and a common vision of the work of the project team.

The particulars of the discussion will be project specific. The focus will be on exploring the boundaries of each individual's mental model for working within a relational model context. What do they know to be true versus what do they believe or assume? One tool to help them see this is to do a **T-Account** or contrasting list of the current rules of the game versus the rules for a possible new way of working. They should also identify, for themselves and the organization, what new possibilities might be available as a result of delivering the project.

Rules of the Game

Control Model	Relational Model
• Leaders give opinions	• Leaders declare commitments
• Analyze what is wrong	• Look for what is missing
• Use what worked before	• Experiment out-of-the-box
• Work to the schedule	• Work to deliver commitments
• Get action approved	• Take responsibility for actions
• Focus on our objectives	• Find mutual objectives

The completed purpose statement's presentation to the leadership team will be the project team's first test of working in a relational way. Does leadership really want to change how business gets done? Is the project team engaged with the performance vision of the leadership team? This first report will test the commitment of both the project team and leadership.

This presentation of the project team's purpose and goals may determine the leadership team's confidence in the project team. (It may also be a test of the authenticity of the leadership team in their commitment to new ways of behaving – do they listen from a commitment to judge or a commitment to support?) The level of confidence will determine the amount of *Space* the project team is given to pursue their project. The bolder the project team is when setting the goals, the more challenge there will be in meeting them. More challenge inherent in the goals should equate to more engagement on the part of the project team. The more engaged the project team, the more confident leadership should be in this project – the more Space the team should be given.

We can confidently predict a first lesson from this initial attempt at doing things differently: communications between the leadership team and the project team will be required, and lots of it, as this project progresses. Every action by the Project Team may be viewed within the context of old behaviors, and thus, interpreted differently than intended. Keep the communications channels open to avoid relational breakdowns.

Link the Individual to the Project

As soon as this initial step of defining Direction is complete for the project team, the role of the project leader transitions to Coaching/Support. The project leader will use individual performance conversations to link the project team's common Direction with each individual's purpose in the form of possibilities. This will ensure that individual actions are consistent with the desired outcomes for the project.

We have seen initial performance conversations go something like this for members of a project team engaged in introducing this relational model:

> **Team Leader**: "So, Jane, you are our accounting expert on this project – tell me why you volunteered to be a member of this team?"
>
> **Team Member**: "Well, I did not exactly volunteer. My boss said that I should do this to get a chance to show what I can do?"
>
> **TL**: "What *are* some of the things you can do for this team?"
>
> **TM**: "I will summarize the expenditures and outputs in a way that makes sense to the other team members in their engineering or sales worlds! Accounting definitions often do not relate well to how non-accountants think in their functional world. I can translate the accounts into something meaningful for them."
>
> **TL**: "So, the team can look for you to show them how to use accounting to help them perform better?"
>
> **TM**: "Yea, something like that."
>
> **TL**: "How did you learn to do that?"
>
> **TM**: "Well, I have kind of always done that. I worked in a manufacturing plant when I was going to school and have always had an interest in understanding cost and production. And I guess I like to see people learn how to use things I know."

TL: "Sounds like you have a passion for coaching others, and it sounds like you use that when you present accounting data. You bring a very useful gift to this team — we have some real cost challenges to meet! I'm glad your boss suggested that you join us."

TM: "Thanks! Yea, I guess I do like to help others learn — that is like coaching. I had not thought of it in quite that way. But it is not like I am an instructor — I don't want to be giving accounting lessons."

TL: "I hear you. You want be a team member who helps others do their jobs better by presenting your work in their context. That is not standing up and telling them how to code expenditures; it is showing them how their coding of expenditures can help them meet our team objectives."

TM: "Yea, thanks for asking me about my contribution. I see this is going to be an opportunity to learn and to show how I can help the team. I might even thank my boss for pushing me to do this project."

TL: "Perhaps I will be the one who thanks your boss. I look forward to learning a bit more about the accounting side myself, and I will be one of your more committed students in learning how to integrate the financial side of the business into everyday decisions. We have an exciting project with a lot of challenge. If we do this well, it could change the way the company does business and provide more opportunities in the future for everyone involved."

This amount of discussion is a heavy initial workload for the project team leader, but ensuring that every member of the team is engaged will lighten the future managing load. You may recall from your management training that it is necessary to focus on results and relationships when planning urgent and critical actions. This conversation is entirely about relationships and results. Building definitions of possibilities that are consistent for the team and individual team members will ensure that their actions support the desired outcome. In combination with linking identity through contribution and establishing individual and collective accountability, *The Performance Connection* for this team is made.

Establish a Accountability System

Just as an Accountability System is one of the four critical elements of the larger organization, it is also a critical element for this first project.

- At the conceptual level, an accountability system is a way of asking every time you undertake an action, "What is the purpose? How will we measure its success?"

- At the process level, an accountability system is a systematic approach to following up targets and actions to manage risk and to provide governance for the project. It is also a procedure to ensure clear accountability and processes for verification – whether self verification by the team or verification by external individuals.

- At the individual level, an accountability system is a performance agreement that is managed using the performance conversation. Individual accountability management also requires the same procedural process to ensure that a clear and common understanding of accountability is maintained.

For this project accountability process, team goals have been linked to the business strategy during the first conversation that gave this team its life. This was a first step in cascading the leadership's performance vision throughout the entire enterprise. These goals were reinforced when the project purpose was established. The individual conversations linking individual purpose to the project vision continued the linking process and started the individual *performance conversations,* which will be a continuing discussion between the leader and each individual as the project progresses. These conversations need to set specific performance goals for each team member, goals linked to the larger picture.

This is as far as we will go with the initial project process, as the key elements are basically present and future steps are project-specific. To this point, the project team has:

- determined their End or *Direction*

- linked the individuals with Purpose, Identity through contribution, and Accountability

- established an accountability process that was linked from the organizational vision through the project to each individual

All of these are key elements for making a performance connection. To complete the picture, the Project Team Leader must continue using the Leadership Practices to develop a *perform-and-learn* context as the work progresses.

From Project to Organization

This initial project introduces the relational model to the organization, and as such, it will generate talk and some stories about doing things differently but no further action without leadership guidance. When leadership wants to move the relational model into the larger organization, the project process, as a model, will have demonstrated some different ways of working. As the relational model is transferred to the larger organization, the key difference is that all supporting organizational process (Human Resources, Finance, Procurement, etc.) will need to be transformed.

Here is an overview of the process for moving the relational model into the organization.

- Establish a compelling reason for introducing the change – what (in terms of performance) do you want this change to accomplish for the enterprise. In other words, write your purpose statement for this transformation, just as the project team wrote a purpose statement.

- Introduce the Relational Management Model to the organization and communicate this purpose using an interactive process whereby each individual must consider what will be different for them. Principles from the *Involve Others in the Conversation* practice should guide this communications event.

- Structure the organization into business-purpose defined units, groups, teams etc. As the project team did, staff each team with complementary skills so that each of these internal enterprises has business capability.

- Introduce each new internal enterprise to the relational model at a working level. Have them write their business purpose, establish performance metrics, and get customer agreement.

- Develop the accountability *Tally Sheet* for the entire enterprise and for each of the business-purpose groups.

- Formalize accountability reviews and integrate them with other standard business practices for your enterprise.

- Coach the organization through the transition phases of dependence, then independence and finally into an interdependent way of seeing Me Inc. and Business Inc. as We Inc.

This, of course, assumes that the Business Inc. vision and strategy is capable of providing guidance for the entire organization. Once leadership understands and commits to the relational model, the capacity of the enterprise's Vision to light the way is the most critical factor for expanding its application beyond the project.

If there are questions about this *Direction* element of the Leadership Model, these questions will probably surface during the project team's presentation of their project purpose statement. In requiring this project team to apply the rule "always look up before you look down to work," you will be asking them to question the connection between their project and the larger organizational vision. If this connection work raised issues for them, it is a signal to take another look at these key pieces of guidance. So, while the project team is learning and teaching others about the impacts, benefits, and changes that will occur as the full relational model develops, the leadership team may wish to be thinking about the organization's *Direction* in the form of a Strategy Review, and that is business as usual – leadership providing strategic direction on an ongoing basis.

Acknowledgements

As many readers will be aware, it takes more than a couple of authors to transform ideas into a readable document of any kind. Our book is no exception. The authors wish to acknowledge a few of the people who contributed to bringing this book to its present stage of life.

This book owes its beginning to Anthony J. Brown, who first suggested that it be written and then continued to guide its development by reading every draft and then gently suggesting improvements until it took enough form that others could grasp its direction and add their contribution. Thank you, Tony for patience and perseverance.

This book owes much of its substance to the teachings of James R. Ewing, who started our tutelage in 1991 and to this day continues to show both authors new ways to bring the human spirit into alignment with business needs. In addition to providing the name for the book, many of the tools used in our relational model were developed by Jim.

As this book moved through its various drafts, the authors had the support and encouragement of many people. In the early days of the book's development, Ken Ehrman, Dave Fisher, Pat Heneghan, and Marcia Ballinger provided invaluable guidance that helped shape the final product. As the concept came together, Margaret Arrowsmith, Keith Davis, Don Duckworth, Alan Giles, Amy Mars, John Morgan, Keith Russell, and Larry Randall reviewed the introductory section and encourage completion of the book. As the manuscript developed, Ronnie Macdonald, Bob Beatson, Richard Lloyd, Andy Parums, and Andy Call provided the feedback that gave the book its final structure.

With a working manuscript in hand, Don Baumgart gave life to several of the concepts through the magic of his sketch pad. We hope you find his sketches amusing as well as informative – we do. Our appreciation is due Michael McIrwin who added much needed clarity to the text, supported our dangling participles, connected split infinitives, and demonstrated the proper use of a colon.

From manuscript to print is still a big step, and one that could not have been completed with out the help of Chris Edwards, Publisher and his crew at Walkerville Publishing. Chris transformed the manuscript, adding the sizzle to the steak, as he likes to say. He and his team integrated graphics, found meaningful lead-in quotes, lifted key thoughts, and birthed a real live book. Thank you: Walkerville Publishing, for demonstrating faith in our work.

And, perhaps the greatest thank you is due the many individuals in our client organizations whom have shared their working experiences and honored us with trust and patience as together we developed and allied the concepts of this relational management model. We learned from each of you and look forward to this book being a catalyst for more learning, together and individually.

Although the words of this book are set in print, applications from the concepts continue to develop and be available though *www.ThePerformance-Connection.org*. A final thank you is due Gemma Anderson for bringing these interactive elements of the book to life though this web site.

Dennis DeWilde is an international business consultant who coaches organizations and executives on how to integrate people with their business strategy as the key to performance improvement. He spent the first decade of his business career in engineering and management positions with American Electric Power, and the second decade as an executive with British Petroleum, before starting his private consulting practice in 1995. He holds a Bachelors of Science degree from South Dakota School of Mines and Technology and a Masters degree from Stanford University Graduate School of Business, where he was a Sloan Fellow. Dennis lives in the Greater Cleveland, Ohio area. He can be contacted via email at:

dmdewilde@aol.com

Geoff Anderson is a consultant, coach and facilitator currently working as Oil and Gas Director of MESA (Middle East Strategy Advisors) in the United Arab Emirates. As a global consultant, Geoff specializes in Change Management, Organization Development, Performance, Supply Chain and Communications. In addition he trains executives in a range of change related topics. Geoff is a lawyer by profession. Since 1978 he has worked mainly in the International Oil Industry but also in the Transport, Energy, Government and Contracting Sectors. His early career was spent with Shell in the UK and Far East and then with BP in Senior Supply Chain and Asset Management roles in both Upstream and Downstream Segments before leaving to establish his own companies, Corporate Fundamentals, ForthRoad and most recently Derson Ltd. Geoff operates between his Dollar, Scotland home and Abu Dhabi and can be contacted via email at:

geoff.anderson@mac.com